T0168356

Notes from Home

Notes
from
Home

20 Canadian Writers Share Their Thoughts of Home

Edited by Cobi Ladner and
the Editors of *CANADIAN HOUSE & HOME* MAGAZINE

Illustrated by Melissa Sweet

McArthur & Company
Toronto

Published in 2002 by McArthur & Company

McArthur & Company
322 King St. West, Suite 402
Toronto, Ontario, M5V 1J2

Copyright © Canadian Home Publishers

All rights reserved. Without limiting the rights under
copyright reserved above, no part of this publication may
be reproduced, stored in or introduced into a retrieval
system, or transmitted, in any form or by any means
(electronic, mechanical, photocopying, recording or otherwise), without the prior written permission of both
the copyright owner and the above publisher of this book.

National Library of Canada Cataloguing in Publication

Notes from home: a collection of essays from the pages of
Canadian house & home magazine/edited by Cobi Ladner;
illustrated by Melissa Sweet.

ISBN 1-55278-319-7

1. Home—Anecdotes. 2. Authors, Canadian
(English)—20th century—Biography. I. Ladner, Cobi
II. Sweet, Melissa

PS8367.H6N68 2002   C818'.5402
C2002-903967-3
PR9197.7.N68 2002

Jacket and interior illustrations: Melissa Sweet
Jacket and interior design: Hambly & Woolley Inc.

Printed in Canada by Friesens

The publisher would like to acknowledge the financial
support of the Government of Canada through the
Book Publishing Industry Development Program (BPIDP)
and the Canada Council for our publishing activities.
The publisher further wishes to acknowledge the
financial support of the Ontario Arts Council for our
publishing program.

10 9 8 7 6 5 4 3 2 1

ACKNOWLEDGEMENTS

This book is dedicated to the talented authors
who shared their personal notes of home with us
each issue.

We would also like to thank Melissa Sweet for
her wonderful watercolours that make each story
come to life,

Barb Woolley and her team at Hambly & Woolley
who always make us look good,

And our publisher, McArthur & Company.

CANADA

CH&H
NFH
2002

PO BOX

NOTES FROM HOME

CH&H
2002

PO BOX

Contents

Not Just a House

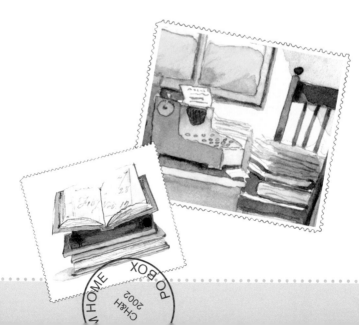

In every issue of *Canadian House & Home* magazine, we show our readers the best in Canadian interior design. We revel in great taste, drool over clever ideas and generally obsess on everything from grand scale to the tiniest details.

But that doesn't mean we forget the difference between a house and a home. Although the words are often interchanged, they are two very different things.

Thankfully, making a home is possible without a house, but, sadly, a house doesn't always make a home. Because a home is about so much more than its decorating, we have included the "Notes from Home" column regularly in our magazine and invite writers who would normally not frequent our pages to tell us their personal accounts — thoughts and experiences we can all share, like moving to the country, clearing out possessions after a parent dies, renovations that just won't end, holiday decorating, first apartments, living abroad, nesting stories happy and sad.

A number of years ago a friend of mine moved away, bought a house with her husband in a small town and began a new life. After two or three years we were talking on the phone and I asked her, "So, do you think you will stay?" Her response was that of frustration: "Why does everyone keep asking me that? When will they realize this is now my home?"

I felt stunned. It's such a personal and elusive thing to know when you are home. I guess I viewed her move to the country as a type of fascinating experiment, and I had to be told, rather bluntly, that she was in fact "home."

We should all be thankful when we find that place. We are acutely aware when we don't have it, when a place is just a place, a temporary shelter until we get to where we yearn to be … home at last.

Cobi Ladner

Cobi Ladner

Editor, *Canadian House & Home* Magazine

Makeshift Living

ELLEN VANSTONE PONDERS HER STRANGE STATE OF
DECORATING PARALYSIS.

My husband and I have a little joke that started
when we used to take driving holidays in the United States. Over the long
distances of the American highways, from California to Rhode Island,
there was nothing we liked better than to talk, listen to music and relax.
Occasionally we'd stop to gawk at weird and fabulous architecture,
from Frank Lloyd Wright's strangely shabby Taliesen West in Arizona to
the Arts and Crafts mansions designed by the Green brothers in Pasadena,
California, to the wooden boat museum in Mystic, Conneticut.

But the one thing we never got around to was shopping for our
various homes over the years. "Oh, look. There's an antique store.
We should stop and look," one of us would say for the 48th time on any
given trip. And whoever was driving would speed up slightly and say,

10

"Hmmm, I dunno. There'll be another one."

After several years of this, we finally did stop at an antique store in New York's Adirondack mountains. It was the sort of quaint, ramshackle outpost that screamed that irresistible siren song of "Charming, under-priced *objets* that will incite ownership pride and the envy of your closest friends for years to come!" but upon closer inspection proved to be a malodorous junk shop run by a silent little man who followed us around with an increasingly menacing air of demented impatience. It was the off-season and utterly, surreally quiet. Circling through the stalls of two-year-old cookie tins and fake Depression glass, I started thinking about the movie *Deliverance* and headed back to the car as quickly as possible without raising suspicion. Max was one step behind me as we slammed the doors and peeled back onto the highway. So now, whenever we want the other one to drive faster, or if we're just looking for a cheap laugh, we say, "Oh, look. There's an antique store. Wanna stop?" This is all very cute and funny, but the point is, we still haven't bought a single thing for the first house we purchased together two years ago.

The house itself is beautiful — a roomy Victorian semi in Toronto's Annex neighbourhood. The previous owner, a funky young architect, restored everything with exacting detail, from mouldings and satiny hard-wood floors to historically accurate foot-high baseboards. He left the walls intact but eliminated a second stairwell and widened doorways to create an overall sense of space and light. Then he married airy Victorian charm with eclectic, postmodern touches: the kitchen has floor-to-ceiling drawers, cupboards and pullout wall trays, all bravely painted chartreuse. Along the stainless steel counters are appliance garages with electrical outlets every six inches. The powder room is tiled to resemble a swimming pool (complete with a "No Diving" mosaic on the wall and a built-in fish tank above the toilet). China cabinets are fitted with the same wavy

glass fronts that cover floor-to-ceiling cabinets on the second-floor landing. The third floor opens onto a deck by way of a glass garage door that
slides up automatically.

All we had to do was install a few light fixtures, throw down some
sisal in the larger rooms, and fill it up with the pieces we'd been admiring
for years at our favourite stores. Instead, two years later, the walls are bare,
lightbulbs dangle from the ceilings, drapery hardware is collecting dust in
its original packaging, and the only bathroom (there are four in all) with
decent lighting still doesn't have a mirror. (I put on my makeup when
I get to work.)

Our failure to decorate has led to the usual domestic conflicts. A spat
over what colour soap to buy for the master bathroom can quickly encom-
pass every disagreement we've ever had, leading us to question both our
relationship and our identity as individuals. We're both acutely conscious
of the fact that how you decorate your home, in the same way as how you
dress or who you marry, is an expression of your identity, revealing both
who you think you are and — inevitably, to the discerning eye — who
you really are. But what's actually stopping us, aside from the usual lack of
time and money, can be explained by my personal theory, applicable
in most situations, that men are stupid and women are insane. And since
I'm writing this and Max is not, let's start with his contribution to our
decorating paralysis.

A successful graphic designer, Max is also a superb carpenter and a
genius when it comes to ideas and architecture and canny real estate pur-
chases. And, like any man who only truly comes alive when surrounded by
power tools in a well-equipped workshop, he's a dreamer. He's in love with
the process. Since our house doesn't have such a workshop (his tools are
crammed into the unrenovated basement rec room, which is pink and
has wall-to-wall carpeting), the process is spread throughout the house.

12

On the main floor, we have pieces of a solid pine harvest table that Max rescued for the cottage from a downtown dumpster — it's been there for months — and a rusted McClary wood stove, also destined for the cottage, also in need of repair and refinishing, and also going nowhere fast. What we actually need in the front hallway is a coat stand, and indeed Max has experimented with making notched pegs using a table saw that he rebuilt himself with original parts from the 1950s. (There is a tiny coat closet there, but since the architect chose pleasing dimensions over functional storage space, it's a useless joke.)

The second-floor landing is adorned with large pieces of metal shelving and brackets that Max is customizing for our walk-in closet. The random metal content of the third floor consists of brushed-aluminum rods and girders that will eventually be used for a modernistic railing with a nautical theme on the back deck.

In the kitchen, between the Sub-Zero fridge and double-oven Paul Bocuse gas stove from France, our microwave is perched on a child's play table about 18 inches off the floor, right where the movers dropped it in 1996. The plan there is for a high-tech butcher-block island with a built-in shelf for the microwave underneath.

A certain lack of commitment is reflected outside the house as well. After a year of dithering, we finally had the massive steel koi pond, fed by a massive steel fountain, removed from the backyard, but haven't quite gotten around to filling in the holes where they once stood.

We do not lack ideas. On the subject of the clothing explosion in our bedroom, for example, I might come up with the notion that it would be super if we installed those shelves and rods in the closet so we could put things away properly. Max agrees wholeheartedly, and takes it 10 steps further — even better would be a customized headboard set out from the wall for side access, fitted with shelves and hooks on the back, tiny

night tables, and nightlights suspended on bent-coil arms that would snake down from the structure with sculptural simplicity. He could build it. Cherrywood. At this point, I look at all the clothes, at the piles of books and magazines sliding along the floor beside our bed, at the muslin rags that are hanging in the windows because Max wants to design the curtain rods himself and have them fabricated by someone he knows, at the picture-free walls that are waiting for us to make frames and cut the mats with the mat cutter he bought me for Christmas. And then I stare silently at Max with a look that makes him think I have deep psychological problems.

Sometime last year, after the noisy arguing stage and before the silent crazy looks stage, I proposed that we hire a handyman to help out with things around the house that Max never had time to do. He took this as a searing attack on his manhood, and answered that maybe he should hire a prostitute to do all the things I didn't have time to get around to. (Hey, if she'll cook dinner, it just might work.)

As for my own part in all of this, I'm not quite sure. Ten years ago I would definitely have pegged it as a classic case of male oppression. He earns more money, he has the power... except that I have no compunction about spending his hard-earned dough. And I'm perfectly free to hit the shops via our line of credit.

So I've had to move on to another theory, about which I've been doing a lot of thinking. I've had time to think because, as I write this, Max is in Maine at a wooden-boat school, learning to build a double-ended lapstrake peapod (which I'm hoping can double as a coffee table in our living room). My original plan was to call our real estate agent the minute he left town and quickly find a better house, one with an enormous workshop and a mudroom so that I can actually have someplace to put the recycling boxes, which now, incidentally, are scattered throughout

14

the house filled with tools, cords and the components of two Muskoka chair kits, while we sit around the barbecue on milk crates.

While I don't blame Max for the lack of a mudroom (for that, I blame the previous owner-architect), I do blame him for his utter lack of self-knowledge when it comes to what kind of person he is, that we are. We are people who relax by beginning projects without wanting the pressure of actually finishing anything, and who should be living in a large studio/workshop instead of a showpiece home that we are ruining with industrial-strength clutter.

But now that he's not around to blame, and I find myself not phoning the real estate agent, I have to admit that there's a lot to be said for pleasing dimensions. The human capacity to adapt to adversity is also at play. The lumber and wood stove have become part of the domestic scenery. I just don't see them anymore. It's the wrong house for us in a number of ways, but it's so charming that familiarity is starting to breed content. It's a home that I'm learning to love, for better or worse, for richer or poorer, with or without light fixtures.

So I must conclude that I also have a role in the failure-to-decorate problem and I may be ready to admit what it is. As much as I joke about Max, the truth is I really value his taste and design sense. I won't go out and do it alone because I want Max to go along with me. To give me his opinions, without thwarting my agenda. And while I wait for the planets to realign themselves so this can happen, I engage in a weird kind of female passivity — waiting for approval, or any other version of demented, stereotypical female behaviour, from Mr. Workshop Guy. After 10 years together, I still think I can, in some way, change him.

Insane.

15

New Christmas

JACOB RICHLER MUSES ON THE INGREDIENTS THAT MAKE A
HOUSE A HOME AND A HOLIDAY GATHERING MEMORABLE.

My girlfriend, Leanne, is crouched in front of the open
refrigerator, perched precariously on her slender haunches. She is holding
a large brown paper-wrapped parcel up over her head, looking for a
cool place to wedge it. But the fridge is small, and already magnificently
overstuffed. As fridge and girl stand off, the package, which contains a
five-pound chunk of raw smoked ham on the bone, one of our Christmas
snacks, begins to leak. Then the dripping blood becomes a stream.
Yet very little makes it past Leanne all the way down to the kitchen floor.

"Leanne!"

Leanne is seven months pregnant and she wears it beautifully. She is
glowing, ebullient. And while pregnancy has not enhanced her alertness,
it has provided her with unshakeable equanimity. When she sees the

16

streaks of blood down her shirt sleeves, and the big wet splotch on her tummy, she drops the bloody ham on the floor and begins to giggle helplessly. I lend her a hand for the struggle back to her feet, and she heads cheerfully downstairs to change. I crouch down to clean up the mess, and I'm thinking, well, how did I get here?

This is December 1997, our first Christmas alone together — Leanne and me, just the two of us in our own home. Before this, Leanne and I lived together in our first place, the one she already occupied when I turned up. It was a fine apartment, but we weren't home much then, and so it took a few months before we realized the place was far too small for the two of us, and gave our notice. With three weeks to spare on the lease, I returned home one evening with a clutch of papers, and we pored over the listings. Not much left, of course, and, by eliminating everything that wasn't very downtown, we came up with a list of three calls to make. I went to see the first place the next afternoon, meeting Leanne afterwards at Betty's pub on King Street, my office local, to tell her about it.

"It's a seven-minute walk from my office at *Saturday Night,* say six-and-a-half from Betty's," I told her. "And your daily cab fare to *The Globe and Mail* would be half the cost of your run from uptown. The main floor — the main room — is one open space, with rough old, wide-plank hardwood floorboards running its length. There's a brick fireplace mid-room, and another in the basement, in the bedroom, which is much like a nest. The bathroom is alongside. There's only one small window down there, sitting level with the sidewalk, on the wall that would be over the bed, but who needs sunlight in the bedroom? At the back of the upper level, there's an open kitchen, with a gas stove, which is perfect for me. A large island chopping block with cupboards underneath juts out from the back wall. And, there's a sliding glass door to the backyard. A grassless, dank backyard. But, but, there is a dishwasher."

"A dishwasher!" Leanne dropped her drink on the bar and gave me a high-five. Of course we took the place.

Soon after we moved in we discovered some idiosyncrasies. Clearly, in the '80s, the place had been owned by some stockbroker who believed in cheap high-tech, or possibly a lighting store salesman. The place was wired. Everywhere one turned, there were switches and sockets and panels and phone jacks. There was a variable-volume control panel for an intercom system, even though the entranceway was in plain view just a foot from the front window. The lights in the backyard had to be activated by a portable remote control. Even the lights in the closets had dimmer switches. The light fixtures, naturally, were hideous, and we quickly removed two flashy pieces of angular glass and chrome that we simply couldn't live with. But we left in place the incongruous design centrepiece in the middle of our main room: a double strip of those Italian track lights that were so popular a decade ago, the ones with the tiny halogen lamps clipped on a wire.

Once a decorator friend had worked out a colour scheme for us and explained where everything had to go, we found that we were living in a spectacular spot for entertaining. It's comfortable here: people are always by for cocktails. Dinner parties are easy, and never a bore for the cook (me), because he's in the same room as the guests with their *apéros*. A fine place for a proper party too, the type that wraps at 6 a.m., the floor sticky with spilt margaritas and crunchy with broken glass. As it happened, we only had one of these.

How things change. The morning after that thirtieth birthday party for Leanne, as I lay in bed recuperating, she went off to the doctor's office and passed a pregnancy test. And so, while I used to spend the Christmas holidays with my family in London, where Leanne joined us our first year together, this year she is too large to manage the flight overseas comfortably. She is, more to the point, too large to endure the flight to London only to there be denied its customary pleasures: mornings passed wandering about museums, afternoons whiled away with improbably long lunches, aimless walks and pub inspections. And, since next Christmas we will be three, and having a family Christmas of our own, this year we have no choice but to stick together in Toronto, and undertake a trial run.

We put the Christmas tree against the front window, where it looks perfect. Our other new Christmas decorations, one pair each of red and green candles, sit handsomely side by side on our dining table. The rest of our Christmas dosh, sensibly, has gone to food and drink, which, as I was brought up, is what this holiday is all about. (I should explain: my mother is Anglican, my father is Jewish, and while my brothers and sisters and I lived at home, we did a Seder and a Christmas celebration. But, it is the latter that endured, if only because the calendar is on its side.)

And so, four days before Christmas, the fridge door can hardly be closed, and there's no place for this bleeding half-ham. I settle on evicting a jar of Mrs. Whyte's pickles from the bottom shelf, shoehorn the meat into its place, and pin it down with the end of a leg of lamb. But I still have to remove a couple more frosty bottles of Heineken to get the door shut. Nice. I'll have one of those, and take a seat.

Everywhere one looks in here speaks of imminent feasts. There is a glorious tower of beer and wine and booze (and, of course, Evian for Leanne) at the end of our kitchen island. A huge pot full of chicken bones and old vegetables is simmering on the stove, stock for a chicken soup and some *soupe à l'oignon gratinée* for the days ahead. The leg of lamb in the fridge is already riddled with little incisions, each stuffed with a sliver of garlic and a pinch of *herbes salées.* The almond pastry crusts are made and resting on the counter. The freezer is bulging with sachets of margarita mix. And a cluster of smoked *chorizo* and *kartnutzel* is dangling from our track lights, which finally proved useful for keeping drying sausage out of the reach of our always-famished cat, Knish, who is now sitting on her hind legs beneath them, howling.

My mother, bless her, surrenders her chestnut stuffing recipe to me over the telephone from London on the day before Christmas, and I pull it off in record time, producing a super roast turkey for Christmas Eve dinner for Leanne's family. The island alongside the dining table serves us well as a carving board. For Christmas, we bake that half-ham, glazed with brown sugar and Madeira. On Boxing Day we somehow squeeze 10 people around the little table for the gigot d'agneau with flageolets. There is cognac, there is Stilton and port and cigars, and no one who passes through, so far as I know, leaves in want of anything tasty to consume.

Now, heading for the New Year, the tower of booze is no longer so impressive. But we can at least fit wine and beer in the fridge again, in between all those leftover roast meats. Such a comforting sight. I am aware of its reassuring presence as I sit here reading one of my Christmas gifts in the chair by the blazing fire. Leanne, defeated again by the weight of her belly, is napping on the sofa, wearing that peaceful expression that comes with a food-filled house.

So, Christmas was effortless. But, of course, it will never be so easy again: next time the holiday table will include a highchair. It appears Leanne and I have outgrown another apartment. We'll miss this little place, and that narrow table wedged into the kitchen, where we sat and ate with so many friends. This was a great flat, and the location was right — it was on people's way. Sure, it was a little shabby, and bums tossed their emptied mickeys into the alcove of our bedroom window. And our first guest here had his car smashed in, his cell phone taken. But he came back again soon after: People have a good time here, they feel welcome.

Hearth & Home

TIMOTHY FINDLEY'S STONE ORCHARD FARM RADIATES WITH
A KITCHEN STOVE AND HEARTY FARE.

For a while our only source of heat at Stone Orchard
was the wood stove in the kitchen. Its pipes snaked through the living-
room and the upstairs bedrooms before reaching the chimney on the roof.
They offered heat to parts of the house — but not enough for writers sitting at their desks. And as winter approached — our first in the house —
we were glad we hadn't put all our money into the down payment. We had
deliberately saved an even thousand dollars for whatever might be essential
to the new home — and so we installed an oil furnace, and simplified the
course of the stovepipe.

We kept the wood stove, however, and for years it served all our
cooking needs — in the kitchen in the winter, and out back in the pantry
during the summer. Its reservoir ensured a constant supply of hot water,

even when storms produced lengthy cuts in our electricity, which would hit both our new pressure pump and water heater. Its oven gave the best possible crust to every loaf of bread — and there has never been anything like the even heat it lent to the frying pan for bacon and perfect eggs. "Awesome eggs," as one of our teenage helpers dubbed them — Saturday chores are always, in our house, sweetened by the prospect of arriving to a full, home-cooked breakfast.

The old stove, however, was not without its hazards. During one of the first visits made to Stone Orchard by my partner Bill Whitehead's parents, we had to spend a day in Toronto. When we got home, we found the parents tight-lipped, shaking — and packed, ready to leave. Nothing we could find to say would persuade them to stay.

Finally, they told us what had happened. In our absence, they had decided to do us the favour of a kitchen clean-up. Scour the sink, scrub the countertops — burn the garbage.

Burn the garbage. Ah, yes.... To this day, we don't know how it happened, but somewhere in the garbage, there had been a can of peas. An unopened can. Into the stove it went, along with the burnables. And out of the stove it came — explosively. The stove lids hit the ceiling — along with what was described as about a ton of soot and ashes. It had taken all day to clean up the mess. All day, except the time it took to pack. Yes, they left the next morning — but after that, their visits were longer — and far more pleasant.

We had our first electric stove on one of those later visits, when Bill's mother taught us a delicious dessert — particularly useful for unexpected company. It was called, simply, Crunch: Into a buttered, ovenproof baking dish (about 10 inches square and 2-1/2 inches deep) pour a can of cherry pie filling and spread it around. Sprinkle a single white cake mix over this, and top with a further sprinkling of about 2/3 cup of sliced almonds.

23

Dribble 2/3 cup of melted butter over all, and bake at 350°F for about 45 minutes. Serve warm with a topping of whipped cream or ice cream.

Youngsters are crazy for it. Oldsters go mad. Midsters, as we were then, sit back and pray the guests don't eat it all. By the way, you can also make it with peach or apple, blueberry or apricot filling — but the best of all is cherry.

My mother's contribution to our "emergency recipes" was also a dessert — and just as simple, just as delicious. Mocha Mousse: In a double boiler, dissolve 24 marshmallows in 1 cup of hot, strong coffee, stirring frequently. Let the mixture cool, and refrigerate until it begins to thicken. Then fold in 1 cup of cream, whipped, and 1 tsp. vanilla. Place into a serving dish and sprinkle the top with 1 grated square of unsweetened chocolate. Chill and serve. And stand back. The stampede may getcha!

There were often times in summer, of course, when neither heat nor hot food could be tolerated — and then, whatever stove it was, we gave it a rest.

This was the time for one of Beverley Roberts's cold soups. Beverley is an old friend from Bill's Saskatoon days. Her gift of the following ultra-simple recipe has remained one of our mainstays, no matter where we are.

Mix equal quantities of cold buttermilk and cold vegetable juice — tomato, clamato or garden cocktail are best. Season with salt and pepper, a squeeze of lemon and a touch of Worcestershire sauce. Pour into a tureen and garnish with fresh herbs (basil seems to work for most juices). Serve with a flourish, pretending — if you like — that it's taken hours to prepare.

Our last stove at Stone Orchard was definitely — and literally — of industrial strength. This was a gas range designed for restaurant use — with a large griddle and a gas broiler called a salamander. The griddle was ideal for feeding breakfast to a houseful of guests — bacon and eggs, pancakes

24

When we got home, we found the parents tight-lipped, shaking — and packed, ready to leave. Nothing we could find to say would persuade them to stay.

and sausage, homefries.... And the salamander did perfect steaks as well as such incredible desserts as crème brûlée. Bill always uses the Alice B. Toklas recipe for the latter, which is basically a custard of egg yolks and cream, slowly cooked and chilled until set and then covered with a centimetre or two of sifted brown sugar. Careful broiling produces a sweet, crunchy top that has to be cracked with the back of a spoon before dessert can be served. Alice knew a thing or two when it came to food. This is a classic.

The griddle was also used for a Stone Orchard specialty, Pork Piccata. I no longer eat veal, so Bill adapted this heavenly Italian dish to either pork or chicken: Cut a pork tenderloin into 1-inch slices. Pound each slice thinly. Bill does this by placing the meat between two empty freezer bags, and pounding it with a wooden mallet. Dredge with seasoned flour and fry in batches — depending on the size of your skillet — about one minute per side, using a very hot mixture of olive oil and butter. When all the meat is cooked and set aside in a covered dish, add a bit more butter to the pan, and enough leftover dredging flour to produce a roux. Deglaze the pan with enough white wine and half as much lemon juice to produce the desired amount of sauce. Cook until slightly thickened, season with salt, pepper and fresh chopped parsley. Reheat the meat in the sauce and serve.

We offer this with basmati rice plus a mountain of zucchini and red pepper strips, sautéed quickly and lightly in olive oil — with or without a touch of garlic.

Over the years, we have settled on a standard menu for larger dinner parties: a whole tenderloin of beef, brushed with a mixture of butter and Kitchen Bouquet seasoning and roasted for about 45 minutes at 500°F. This produces a roast both rare and medium rare. In annington, we have been extremely lucky to have Ron Butterworth as our butcher. His pork and beef are exemplary — the beef among the best we've ever had. We serve it accompanied by sliced potatoes cooked (oven or microwave) in olive oil with a lot of garlic. The green vegetable is usually a blend of two purées: spinach and parsnip, seasoned with lots of butter, salt, pepper and a bit of nutmeg.

One of our most memorable dinners was served on Canada Day, July 1, 1985. When we were about to set the table, we discovered that with house guests and other visitors — including our current teenage helper, Barry Spence, and his entire family — there would be thirteen at table. This made everyone uneasy until we remembered we had the perfect additional guest for that particular day. He usually sat in my bedroom in the form of a stunning ventriloquist's doll — a memento from a play I had written for Bill Hutt, who played the title role: John A. Macdonald. And so, we set that extra place and enjoyed our celebratory beef in the company of our first prime minister.

Making Change

SANDRA SHAMAS SPRING CLEANS AT HER FARM WITH A
HEALTHY DOSE OF HUMOUR.

It's around this time of year that I get that old "feeling." Oh, I know what you're thinking: "Spring, and a young girl's fancy turns to..." Now just cut that out! While it may be true that animals on farms and fish in streams are enjoying themselves and each other, in the warmth of the spring sun, my fancy turns to spring cleaning.

I'm not sure when the "feeling" starts. My best guess is late February, when all that groundhog action takes place. It starts slowly; first my skin feels too tight ... like I took a bath and my skin shrunk, and now I gotta walk around in a suit of skin that's bugging me, 24 hours a day. This is around the time I think I should start a new eating regime, work out more, get manicures, or just moisturize myself into a stupor. It's safe to say I'm distracted, and slightly irritable.

Then I notice how much I hate my clothes. The colours are wrong, the textures are scratchy, and I have nothing to wear. And, even if I do manage to pull together some outfit that will ensure I'm not driving naked down the 401, I have no shoes. All my footwear seems to be against me. No matter how much effort I make to maintain my suede shoes, they always reach a point of no return.

A sidebar to all this extraordinary annoyance is that my hair is wrong. It's in the right place, and I'm grateful for having hair on my head, but past that — it's not doing me any favours. "Naturally curly" means, "I'll do any damn thing up here that I please, and you'll just have to find the strength of character to walk with me in public." For reasons that are still being researched, it creates a part that goes not front to back, but from ear to ear. Then the whole front part (like a room divided to sing a song in rounds) curls forward. One, big, giant curl. Surfers find it attractive. Luckily, I live on a farm, so that no one else can hear the screaming.

There's about a month of this festive activity during which I do not manage to alleviate my own distress. In fact, it seems I do everything to exacerbate the symptoms: I don't drink enough water, I take drying show-ers, and forget to moisturize. Then I solve my wardrobe dilemma, and start wearing the same three pieces of clothes, like a uniform. Finally, I rationalize that my hair and I are just going through some phase that will surely end when I shave my head. I think I've got 'er licked, and then I get the "feeling."

It happens real quiet like. I'm sitting having coffee, in the same chair that I've been sitting and having coffee in for, oh, 8 to 10 years. I shift my weight from one side to another. I cross and uncross my legs. I'm really uncomfortable. I get up, turn around, and stare at it like I've never seen it before. As in, how did this "stranger" get into my house? I shoot a ques-tioning stare at the other chairs. They're understandably quiet; in fact,

some are making it a point to avoid my eyes. I start walking through the house. It's starting to dawn on me: I walk by my armchair, and suddenly see, as if for the first time, that the side table is way too high! I've practically had to fully extend my arm upward to put my coffee cup down. It becomes quite clear to me that the vintage armchair, the overstuffed couch, and Persian rug from Home Depot, just don't look right together. I've been in denial. What's wrong with having three tables in the front office? So what if they're all against the window, and the groovy office chair doesn't fit under any of them?

The foyer is no better. I have a side chair in the corner, for putting on shoes and talking on the phone, but I never sit in it. Why? Because the springs are gone, and it's depressingly uncomfortable. I run from room to room, seeing how "make-do" everything seems. The evidence continues to support the diagnosis; I don't know what I'm doing. How did this happen? Did I purchase all my furniture in a trance, and arrange it while on tranquilizers?

Then it hits me: I don't like any of my furniture! Amidst the panic, a moment of calm ... I know what to do, it's crystal clear ... I'll collect all my furniture, throw it into a big pile in the front yard, buy a bag of marshmallows, and light the whole geezly mess on fire. Maybe I'll throw my clothes on the pyre for good measure.

Oh, the sinking feeling, that I'm sharing my home with things that I'm not "in love" with anymore. I share my heartache with my neighbour Kara, whose beautiful home suits her family to a tee. The colours are right, stuff matches, there's a sense of comfort. I tell her that my relationship with quarter-sawn oak is over. That I can never look at down-filled furniture again. She listens, pours tea, and lovingly says, "Talk to Nancy."

Enter Nancy Nevile-Smith, a friend and interior designer. I call Nancy. I talk, she listens. I'm sure I am not the first person to call and bend her ear with sad stories like, "It looked so perfect in the store, it was on sale, I had to have it. When I brought it home it (1) took over my house, (2) made me write bad cheques, (3) ate the dog (pick one or more). When I tell her my plan to burn my furniture, she senses my desperation. "I'll drop by and have a look," she says. I breathe a sigh of relief. I can feel the skin stretching a little more comfortably across my forehead. Help is on the way.

And help she does. Nancy's not in my house more than 10 minutes when she asks about the piano. "Do you play?" No. "Why is it in the kitchen?" Good question. "You need more light near your reading chair," she observes. I stand there stunned, slack-jawed, as if I've witnessed a miracle. Of course. Light! Go toward the light! Her suggestions are simple, and encourage me to believe that they will make a vast difference in the movement, comfort and hospitality of my home. On her way out, Nancy says, "Let's start with small stuff you can do yourself. If you get stuck, give me a call."

The next day finds me calling my contractor for estimates on a new surround for the tub. There's a spring in my step and new space in my outlook. I never thought I'd say this: what a relief to know I can always change for the better.

When I call to regale Nancy with my efforts, I tell her the piano has found a new home where it will be played and appreciated. She asks me what I want to do with the newfound space. "I don't know, a hutch, or a cabinet or something…" I can hear her patiently listening to my indecisive blathering. Then she says, "Sandra, let me help you find the right thing." I hear the underlying message. "Sure, Nancy, can't wait!"

Ah, spring. I have a new lease on life. I'm reborn. Even my hair seems happy.

Of Things Past

ANNE KINGSTON SORTS THROUGH A HOUSEHOLD OF
CHILDHOOD MEMORIES AT HER FAMILY HOME.

My brother David lifts the Kissing Bear from the
cabinet on the left side of the fireplace. The Orrefors figure fits snugly
in the palm of his hand. My mother bought it in Copenhagen. I remember
her unwrapping it, this quirky round bear fashioned from rippled glass
as opaque as ice. How it came to be known as the Kissing Bear, I can't remember. Like so many things that make up the mythologies that connect
every family, it just was. "Who wants this?" David asks. There is silence.
The bear belongs here, in my mother's living room. But that isn't an option.

The three of us have been at the emotionally exhausting task of clear-
ing out my mother's house for days. It has been two months since she died.
We've put it off, but can't any longer — the house has been sold. Finally
Rob, my youngest brother, speaks. "If nobody else wants it, I'll take it."

Now what? We look around. The brass candlesticks on the mantel? The carved owl that always sat on the bookcase? The stereo? The exercise has that surreal quality that seems to govern events that happen only once in one's life. As we go about dismantling the stage set on which our lives have played out, it begins to feel as if we're taking part in some kind of metaphysical garage sale, rummaging around for souvenirs from another lifetime.

How strange it is to take objects that were once a part of everyday rituals and view them in a new context — which is really no context at all. Just how do you go about divvying up the Christmas ornaments that always adorned one tree? There are also practical considerations — we all have our own homes, our own families; we don't have room for all of it — and we were raised not to put too much stock in possessions. My mother was of Irish heritage, and had a sardonic fatalism that surfaced from time to time. She spoke more than once of not cluttering up the house with junk we'd have to rummage through when she was dead. "Mum," we would wail, "don't say that," unable to handle the thought of it.

We still can't. I want to believe my memories of and love for my mother have no connection to these things, but now they are all we have left of her. And as we sort through them, it becomes clear how much the house reflects not only her taste but her spirit. It is so much like her — understated, ordered, yet warm and generous and welcoming. There is comfort here still.

She had moved into the house in the early 1970s, after she married our stepfather. Before that we lived in the house she had bought with our father, who died when we were small. That house was always a sad place for her, but this one had contained much happiness. She had made it light, airy and comfortable. She liked nice things; they represented the distance she had travelled from a hardscrabble childhood. She lived here alone for a decade after my stepfather's death. Then she became ill. She fought that battle for months, fiercely raging against the thought of losing her independence, of which her house was a big part.

My mother had left virtually no instructions for what we were to do with things. All she asked was that her nieces and close friends pick a teacup from her collection. It was the perfect memento of her, modestly appropriate: a cup of tea was her antidote for life's ills. And she was right. Everything always seemed better after a cup of tea.

She expected we would never fight over her possessions, and we don't, even though there are things we all want. We intuitively know what belongs with whom. I am the eldest and the only girl, so, though it is foreign to me, it's fitting that I take my great-grandmother's rarely used fine white china with the gold rims. Rob takes the inexpensive everyday blue and white china. Though less grand, it has far more meaning for us, and, in the years that follow, I always feel a pang when I see it in his house. Rob also took the piano. That seemed right; he spent the most hours playing it. It was understood that David would have the print my father bought at a used bookstore, of a round blonde child sitting in a highchair, because it looked like David as a baby. David also wanted a cast-iron toy train and car that had belonged to my father; these things are some of the only links to a man he barely remembers.

The care my mother took with everyone and everything in her life is evident everywhere. A place for everything, and everything in its place, she would tell us. But it wasn't until we were in the house those last times that the significance of that was apparent. As children with one parent, our lives often felt precarious, but we always knew thread and needle could be found in the sewing drawer in her bedroom, that there was always apple juice in the downstairs pantry. Even now, in her final act of generosity, everything is organized. She had made this as easy as it can be.

There was no place in my mother's life, or her home, for frills or

clutter or false sentiment. Her choice was always for the simple, the spare, the clean-lined, like her three-seater Parson-style sofa, bought over 30 years ago at Avon Galleries at the now-defunct Simpsons department store. My mother bought good things, not because she was extravagant, but because she was frugal, having been raised in a family where thrift was a necessity as much as a virtue. "Buy the best you can afford," she always said. "That way you won't have to worry about replacing it so soon."

She always had definite ideas of what was right and what wasn't. Yet her taste often veered into the unconventional. Her preference was often for the eclectic and quirky, and these are the things that have the most resonance for us. The art that covered the walls, for instance, was an odd combination that somehow looked right because it was chosen with passion and enthusiasm. There are framed pen-and-ink Christmas cards sent by an artist friend, an Australian fern matted with gold velvet in a wooden frame. Amid it all there are our own childish efforts — an abstract water-colour Rob painted when he was 5; a macramé wall hanging I did when I was about 11 that is very ugly but went up in the hallway nonetheless.

"Don't have to ask who's getting this," Rob jokes as he takes the macramé off the wall, handing it to me. The three of us have not been alone in the house like this since we were teenagers, and have quickly fallen into caustic, adolescent banter. When we come across an awful oil painting my mother and stepfather were given as a wedding gift, stashed in a basement closet, we howl with laughter. Before the artist, a family friend, came to visit, my stepfather used to make a production of hanging it in a prominent place, taking it down again when she left.

We discover that we remember different things about our childhoods, that it wasn't the shared experience we thought. Different things have different meanings for each of us. Rob wants a pale blue mixing bowl with an omelet recipe inscribed in German on one side, David the soft beige

35

wool tam and scarf my mother often wore, and an Albrecht Dürer print of an owl. I take the worn blue sweatshirt she gardened in, and a poster of a botanical drawing of an artichoke that hung by the side door.

We're surprised by how much we care about the smallest items in the kitchen — beat-up measuring spoons, juice glasses, tea towels, a spoon rest shaped like a daisy. We pore over an old recipe file and come across the recipe for the Santa Claus cake that went on the mantel every Christmas. There's an odd solace in the continuity of using the same teapot, the same pans, cookie sheets and appliances, like the old black-and-white KitchenAid mixer that made hundreds of batters for muffins and cakes.

My mother named things, which gave them an almost mythic significance. A kitchen spoon with a swirl at the tip was known as the Magic Spoon because we believed it made food taste better. A green hot water bottle was known as Mr. Hot Water Bottle. Then there was the Southern Belle, a brass bell shaped like a woman wearing a bonnet and crinoline. When we were sick, Mum would place it at our bedsides to ring if we needed her. At other times, the bell sat on the oak drop-front desk in the second floor hallway. As family lore had it, the desk had been purchased by my grandmother from the Eaton's catalogue for $25.

Going through the bank of drawers that line one wall in her bedroom is difficult. Those that contain clothing are the least so; the jewellery drawers, which still house trinkets we had bought her as children, are harder. Some of it will go to my brother's daughters, who are so young they will remember her no other way. The most difficult to deal with are those filled with paper. Some offer reminders of her life before us, which is intriguing since my mother didn't talk much about her childhood. There's the newspaper clipping that announced she had won a scholarship to high school. There are reminders of her life as a young teacher, travelling with friends to holiday in Miami. A cartoon from the artist James G. Reidford, a friend of my father's, depicting my father and mother waiting at a bus stop, with the caption "Al and Marg goin' dancin'" underneath.

Some things we uncover are startlingly heartbreaking: a stack of birthday and Mother's Day cards we had given her, revealing handwriting in varying degrees of maturity, carefully tied with a ribbon in the back of one drawer. In the same drawer, I am surprised to find almost all of my published writing neatly cut out and folded. "How did she do that?" I wonder. I don't maintain such a complete set of clippings.

My mother was primary custodian of our family history, a responsibility she undertook with her characteristic prudence. She kept everything — baby cards, diaries from grade school, report cards, photographs, notebooks. In her bedroom hang three photographs, one of each of us, taken at the same time. I am seven, David is five and Rob three. They are a set: the frames are identical; we look young, happy, innocent. We each take our own picture, silently recognizing the symbolism: our mother was the anchor; without her, what was going to happen? This is the hardest part, as we move from room to room, completing what seems to be an endless task. We are dismantling the place we assumed would always be there. The ache of grief, ironically, keeps us from that truth. In the years ahead we will regret how quickly we went through things, and realize that we might have missed things, even wasted things, which to my mother would have been the greatest sin. This was a woman who wouldn't throw out water used to steam vegetables, but froze it to use for soups and stocks.

Friends, family and Goodwill take what they can use. The sofa goes. Someone takes the dining room set. Where it ends up none of us remember, though it won't be in a room filled with the Blue Willow dishes my mother treasured. That makes me sad. But it will be in another room, a setting for another family's memories. That is good. There are more than enough of those still to sort through here.

Anne Kingston

Building Blocks

LINDA FRUM SURVIVES AN ENDLESS RENOVATION WITH A HOUSE
FULL OF POWER TOOLS AND TWO INQUISITIVE TODDLERS.

At the start of the first-floor renovation of the
Cape Cod-style house I share with my five-year-old twins, my interior
designer, Sasha, made an encouraging joke. "Don't worry, Linda," he said.
"The good news is that you're already divorced, so there's no fear that the
renovation will destroy your marriage."

We both found this very amusing. But Sasha's little joke only managed to prove the rule by which I live: It's never the problem you're expecting that ruins you, it's the one you're least expecting. Who would have
guessed that my contractor's marriage would collapse mid-renovation,
causing major delays to the project, and heartache for us both?

Stories of incompetent, elusive contractors are, of course, nothing
special, something I learned when I complained about my situation to

38

friends, only to find myself engaged in bizarre games of one-upmanship.

"Your contractor is having a nervous breakdown?" said one friend dismissively. "I know a case where a contractor died. On site. Before the roof was completed. The clients discovered him when they returned from their honeymoon."

OK. I couldn't top that.

But even if my contractor problems were not the worst of all time, they were still tricky. It was partly my own fault. I was utterly ineffectual at throwing the necessary hissy-fits contractors seem to require to stay motivated.

"The contractor can't come to work today," I would tell Sasha. "It's his daughter's birthday, and, with his divorce and all, well, he really needs to be there, poor guy..."

"Didn't he tell you it was his daughter's birthday two months ago?" Sasha would demand.

"Wha — ooh! Man, that's rude!"

"Tell him his behaviour is utterly unacceptable. Yell at him!"

"But if I yell at him, won't he show up even less? Anyway, I don't like yelling at people. Do I have to?"

It took me a while to catch on that, yes, contractors only respect you if you're evil with them.

We had moved into a small apartment next to some railway tracks in the optimistic but delusional hope that the kids (only two years old at the time) might think two months of "camping out" would be (wheee!) fun. The decor of the apartment was very simple. Three mattresses tossed on the floor. A TV set, also on the floor. One suitcase of clothing each. Later, piles of clothing on the floor.

I called this dingy, depressing apartment (selected because it was cheap, and only a few blocks from our house) our "playhouse."

"Isn't this fun?" I would say to the children enthusiastically. "Our own playhouse! The size of a real apartment. We're so lucky!" They, however, didn't find it fortunate that a little grey mouse lived in the hallway outside our door, nor that a train passed by the window every 15 minutes, rendering conversation (and, more importantly, the TV) inaudible.

"We don't like it here," said Barbara and Sam, with the characteristic frankness of two-year-olds. "Why can't we just live at home?"

"Because our house is too messy right now," I would explain brightly.

Soon they took to greeting strangers with this piece of interesting news: "Hi. Our house is very messy. We can't live there." My general appearance during that time — rumpled clothes rescued from the piles on the floor — did nothing to mitigate the suggestion that I was anything but an extremely slothful mother.

The renovation was supposed to last 3 months. It took more than 12. We moved back into the house after only 2 of those 12 months had passed. It was probably unwise, but the three of us couldn't bear the "playhouse" any longer. True, back at the house the staircase to the second floor was incomplete, creating a potential death spiral. There was no kitchen, so meals had to be takeout, consumed en famille in my bedroom. A ferocious raccoon was staking out squatter's rights in our windowless dining room. And these were just the easy problems.

But were we unhappy?

Not a bit.

For the children, who could never quite figure out what was wrong with our house in the first place, the renovation represented a constant stream of intriguing strangers weighed down by even more intriguing power tools. And as every mother knows, children would much rather play with a real 10-speed drill than some plastic thing that only pretends to be dangerous. Quite simply, they were in heaven. Our house was filled with power saws, sledgehammers, nailguns, and toxic glues. In other words, toys, toys, toys!

As for me, like all renovators before me I was tranquilized by the grotesque orgy of shopping required to get the job done.

By my side throughout the whole ordeal was Sasha. A sympathetic and wise presence. A voice of experience. A moderating force. Before he was my designer, he was already my friend. But during the period that it took to complete the renovation, he also took on the roles of shrink and surrogate husband. (In the emotional rather than physical sense. Even Sasha has his limits.)

Perhaps this range of service is not typically available to the clients of interior designers. But it should be. It was to Sasha that I cried each time my contractor failed to show up. (And it was Sasha who finally agreed that since I was never going to do it, he would have to get evil with him.) It was to Sasha that I complained when the appliance supplier told me there would be another three-month delay in delivery of my Australian oven. ("Who ever heard of an Australian oven?!" my father demanded when I mentioned it to him. "What will happen when your Australian oven breaks? Where will you get an Australian oven fixed?!" A very perceptive man, my father, a very perceptive man.) And it was to Sasha that I would say, "Let's go shopping."

Before the renovation, I had thought of shopping as a highly private and personal activity. I had faith in my own good taste and bargaining instincts. But the months spent shopping with Sasha taught me otherwise. Unaccustomed to shopping with someone at my elbow, it took time for Sasha and me to find our rhythm. In the beginning I would hold up a bolt of fabric and exclaim with joy, "This is it! I love this! It's gorgeous! I'm going to do the whole room in this." And Sasha would say demurely, "Of course, it's your decision, but why don't we keep looking?"

41

At first I would overrule him. I would buy the lamp that he said was too small for the space, and bring it home defiantly, only to discover that it was ... too small for the space. But since he didn't gloat about it, and I began to accept that I didn't know as much about design as I thought I did, our relationship not only survived but thrived.

Eventually, Sasha developed a handy phrase to deal with my enthusiasms. I would point to a lamp, or a rug, or a side table, and say tentatively, "How pretty?"

And he would say, "You can't have it."

This spared me saying, "I love it," and him saying, "It's ugly." And it was a very good system.

When the house was finally completed, the results were far more beautiful than anything I had dared hope for. Like the other important projects of my life — having children and writing books — renovation seemed to fit into the category of a creative act, painful to deliver but worth every dint of effort.

All the inconveniences now seem like a distant dream, as Sasha promised they would. All that's left is pleasure. At least that's how I see it. But I'm beginning to suspect my children remember it differently. When I recently mentioned that maybe it was time to fix up the third floor, they looked at each other and burst into tears.

"I want to build bedrooms for you guys in the attic!" I said, not anticipating the Brothers Grimm implications.

"But we're good children!" they wailed.

Dear little ones. I suppose the next round of renovations can wait.

LINDA FRUM

Building Blocks

NOTES FROM

43

Homes Away

KAREN LAWRENCE DISCOVERS THAT HOME IS WHERE YOU MAKE IT AFTER LIVING IN SOUTHERN CALIFORNIA FOR TWO DECADES.

It's been 20 years since I moved to California from rural Alberta. This seems incredible to me — I've lived here longer than I lived at home with my parents. A friend in Toronto, someone I haven't seen since high school, writes, "I envy you San Diego for its beaches, warmth and beautiful people. Are you at home there? If not, why live in a place that is not home?" So big, so crowded, so hectic, so — American.

Why indeed? There's something kind of wrong about it, isn't there? These silly palm trees, the crashing surf, the aroma of a million hamburgers sizzling on backyard grills — I guess it is pretty juvenile to live in a place that's a vacation destination. If I were a real adult, wouldn't I get a job at the Regina Public Library, use my crockpot more often, shovel some money into an RRSP? I'd at least own a winter coat — I'm a Canadian.

44

"You have no conflict in your life," grumbles another friend over the phone from Washington, D.C. Well, maybe on the outside that appears to be true. The lack of seasons can cause some pretty serious dislocation on the time/space continuum. Living in a perfect climate day in, day out, you do kind of lose your edge. Real discipline is required to stay indoors and get any work done — I mean, if you work at a desk and not a skateboard rental shop. Having children helps somewhat, because they need school supplies in September, immunizations and birthday gifts at very specific times, and their long break is called, like everywhere else, Summer Holidays. But they wear shorts all year. At least boys do. Maybe black, formal shorts for a wedding or funeral, but shorts, definitely. We adults learn to live with a persistent, vague uneasiness. Isn't there something I should be doing? Then suddenly, wham! Ten years have gone by. Maybe this is a consequence of aging, and it would be happening if I still lived in Windsor, Ontario. I have no way of knowing. When I lived in Edmonton and spring rolled around, I knew what I was supposed to do. Around Victoria Day the snow started melting, and you got on with it. Take off snow tires, put up screens, take off long underwear, start shaving under-arms again, wash car and see what colour it is. Here, you find yourself drifting into remembrance of things past when you smell freshly cut grass — the day after Christmas. I'll never get used to that, cutting the lawn by the glow of the Christmas lights on the porch.

Like I said, it's just wrong.

I never meant to stay this long.

My first home in California was oddly beautiful: a crumbling old mansion with a dozen bedrooms, five baths, and an enormous cracked swimming pool sitting on the edge of a eucalyptus canyon, with distant views of the Pacific. How I loved that place! It was filled with the ghosts of grander times — elegant parties, formal gardens, breakfasts on the terrace,

45

maids awaiting. In 1978, the Villa Dilapidada, as we called it, housed a core troupe of seven or eight twentysomethings and a changing cast of friends, lovers, children and visitors. I had come to California to study, to write, to get away from winter, to start a new life with what I could pack into my Toyota Corolla: clothes, typewriter, books, my yellow Birkenstocks (which came unglued in the 110-degree heat outside Bakersfield). Everybody was from somewhere else; I wasn't the only resident alien. None of us had any furniture besides our foamies and oddments scrounged at thrift stores. But in those days you could decorate with a lace tablecloth for a bedspread, a jumble of floor pillows and lots of incense.

That empty old beauty was our theatre, our lives the play. We Villans lived peaks and valleys — explosive love affairs, sudden dashes to Hawaii or Mexico, devastated bank accounts, midnight tarot card readings — any of which seemed more cataclysmic than the occasional earthquakes our nervous relatives called about. What earthquake? I was getting psycho-structurally balanced yesterday. We hosted raw foods banquets, tai chi classes, weddings, tantric workshops, theatre rehearsals, horrific Halloween parties. One roommate, who called herself the Reverend Laura Lou Lowy, held impromptu séances with diverse spirits on various balconies around the house, the ends of her filmy pink and lavender scarves, skirts and shawls mysteriously wafting around a corner like smoke as you entered a room, her imperturbable smile still hanging in the air like the Cheshire Cat's. Spirituality, raw foods, lithium … we never knew what alchemy created that smile.

I was in something of a goddess phase myself. My room had high ceilings, white walls, a white Flokati rug, a private bath and a western view of treetops in the morning fog. I was a different person in that room than I had ever been anywhere else; it was my first real "room of one's own."

Walking up the broad wooden stairs and into my room, I felt embraced by a welcoming distinctly feminine spirit: cool and clear as moonlight, a pool of serenity. My desk was a simple rectangle of glass across two black filing cabinets. I sat there and looked out to the ocean, to Japan, and wrote in my journals: poems and dreams and pieces of what would later become my first novel. In that room, I first kissed the man I would marry years later. The room itself invited people: it housed all sorts of rituals — for the full moon, a roommate's wedding, the opening of a friend's play. We were, I guess, trying to bring back older ways in our search for the new, for our truest, best selves, our true loves, our life's work.

Once a month I drove up to Los Angeles to teach. Those were exhilarating trips: young and single, driving through the Hollywood Hills toward the ocean on a starry December night, with the windows down and the heater on, thinking, My God, I'm here, it will never get better than this. San Diego seemed almost rustic compared to L.A. — it still does, which has definite advantages. L.A. offered good theatre, great restaurants and world-class nutcases, who have long been a cliché. If I hadn't learned to drive in Detroit I'd never have had the courage for those freeways. My route was always scribbled on the back of an envelope — "5N to 405N to 10W to 101N" — which sometimes didn't help, because at 75 miles per hour I'd suddenly be whizzing under a sign, my sign, the one I needed to tell me where to go – that announced, inexplicably, Golden State Freeway, Harbor Freeway, Ventura Freeway. No number, no "N," no nothing. I always made sure my tank was full, so I wouldn't be stuck gasless in Funkytown somewhere. I still do this. It's cheap insurance.

Much that was L.A. in those days seemed fresh and exciting. The breezy anonymity, a sense of limitless possibility, a post-est zing to the slightest of encounters. A friend who had gotten out of the movie business and into body lotion had a shop on Melrose, which was just aborning as

47

the Via Sacra of hip. Here I stocked up on her potions and powders, picked up a turquoise shirt or some earrings at Fred Segal, zoomed over for coffee and baklava at Café Figaro, then stopped in at the Bodhi Tree for a book on how to transcend the body. Anoint, adorn, feed, transcend — you could do it all in a few short blocks. If you could find parking.

And now? Well, the Villa was demolished and a gated condominium complex erected on that lovely canyon. I moved a few miles away, to a home my husband and I came to as newlyweds nearly 17 years ago. We remodelled, restored and rewired every inch of this 85-year-old Craftsman bungalow, room by room. And though we talk often about moving — to another state, another country even — we'd find it terribly hard to leave: not San Diego, but our home, which has embedded itself in our lives in ways I never imagined. When I brought my newborn son home, I carried him through these rooms, showing him pictures, the garden, his crib, whispering in his tiny ear, "This is where you will live now." We've lived here so long we've had four sets of neighbours next door. We've had garden parties and Christmas feasts, sleepovers and bubble-baths, and ever so many wonderful dinners in this house; each room has its stories and memories, layered like the paint on the wall.

I realized some time ago that there is no perfect place to live. Yes, in California we have bad schools, senseless crime and congestion. But friends across Canada tell me of problems there too, if of a different nature or magnitude. All our lives have been invaded by materialism, low culture and bad manners; keeping those aspects of modern times at bay may have more to do with how we live than where. Canada, California — you find home with those you love, where you can work and live by your values.

Or, perhaps, home finds you.

48

Cold Comforts

RUSSELL SMITH RECALLS THE FRIGID STUDENT LODGINGS AND
RAIN-SOAKED FRENCH LANDSCAPE THAT STOKED A PASSION
FOR THE WRITTEN WORD.

A great deal of French poetry is about rain.

Rain, melancholy, autumn, rain. Lines that drum softly. Lines that hiss and
splash. Grey horizons, slick streets. Lines that play on the similar sounds of
the words for "rain" and "cry": *Il pleure dans mon coeur/ Comme il pleut sur
la ville.*

I lived in a grey stone house at the base of a sheer cliff, under the
city walls of a medieval French town, and read this poetry in the grey light
of the tall window in my room. I would wrap myself in sweaters and
wrap my hands around mugs of tea that I would boil up on the gas camp
stove on the wooden table at the centre of my room, a table that was
desk and kitchen, and look through the blurry glass at the heavy sky, the
rain as it softened the muddy road and patterned the green river across the

50

road, and I would look back down at my book and read, *Oh! l'automne l'automne a fait mourir l'été / Dans le brouillard s'en vont deux silhouettes grises.* (Oh! Autumn autumn has made the summer die / In the fog two grey silhouettes are departing.)

I remember reading the philosopher poet Francis Ponge, who devotes an entire page of obsessive prose to the patterns of rain on a courtyard. "In the middle it is a delicate and threadbare curtain (or a net), an implacable but relatively slow descent of quite small drops, a sempiternal precipitation lacking vigor, an intense fragment of the pure meteor." This is how the French think. I would stand up and go to the cracked window with its weathered wooden shutters and look down at the muddy garden and the sullen green river and think: I want to be able to do that too.

I was lonely there. I had graduated from high school in Halifax, Nova Scotia, and accepted my father's instruction (and financing) to live for a year abroad before attending university in Canada. We had picked this sleepy town from a series of brochures. The town was Poitiers, in the central west, a town of grey stone with a university and Roman ruins and a sunken Romanesque cathedral. The university is one of the oldest in existence, anywhere, but in the 1960s they moved the students out of the half-timbered medieval buildings, to a grim postwar campus in a distant suburb, a Stalinist camp of vast open spaces and crumbling concrete blocks. This was my first view of university: a cinder-block residence in a field of rubble — in rain. I spent almost a week in my cell there, with my two enormous suitcases, jet-lagged and petrified, listening to political disputes in Arabic through the walls.

I found an apartment despite the Gallic squealing and Pentagon-level bureaucracy of the student housing service. I took the first landlord that would have me: a man as bent and wrinkled as his stubby vines. His house at the base of the cliff dated from about the mid-19th century, grey and

51

austere. Every surface was bare: tile or stone floors, stucco walls. There was a dark wooden staircase that he would wax weekly. The tiled entrance hall where my mail would be stacked was cool and dim and smelled of wax and disinfectant.

He worked in his garden all day, where there were pears, apples, grapes, a rooster and a rabbit hutch, and in the evening watched the television, turned to a hysterical volume, in the kitchen. He would sleep at 10, and then a thick rural silence would descend.

There were two rooms for rent in the house: a couple of French students had the prize one on the second floor. I was given the back room on the ground floor, the one right against the cliff face. Out one window I saw stone; I could not see the city wall high above me, at the top of the cliff, but I knew it hung up there, excluding me. The stone walls of my room were papered over with massive pink flowers. I hung my clothes in a plastic wardrobe printed with slightly smaller but equally pink flowers. I had a single bed, two narrow wooden tables — one for writing, one for cooking — and a lamp made from a bottle filled with sand. There was a small hooked rug on the stone floor. There was no phone. I went to the supermarket to buy my gas camp stove, a pot and an electric kettle.

There was no other heat at all. My parents sent me parcels of blankets and sweaters from Canada. My landlord shyly asked for the exotic stamps, to give to his grandchild.

The French students and I shared a bathroom. The first time I ran into the rather hirsute young man on the polished wooden stairs, he greeted me and told me that there was a problem with hot water in the house; it would not support two baths in a day, so we would have to work out a schedule. Fine, I told him, you tell me which days you want. Well, he said, since I was here first, I'd like to stick to my current schedule: I take a bath every Thursday.

I told him I did not think that was excessive.

The student couple moved out in midwinter, and the old man offered the prize room to me, the room with the big window on the garden, the river, the sawmill on the opposite bank. The departing students said it was slightly warmer, but they were wrong. It had a wooden armoire, and only one table, and a bricked-in fireplace with an intractable red "STP" sticker dead centre. The wallpaper was grey flowers.

A poor Turk moved into the frozen cave downstairs. He smoked cigarettes that seemed to be made of a kind of super-concentrated dung.

To get to my classes in the Stalinist suburb, I walked down the dirt road, along the river, climbed stone stairs built into the cliff — about a hundred — and took a bus at the top. At school I sat in the frigid classrooms with students and professors who all smoked, and learned a language through a literature that seemed to be all about rain. In the quietude of this life, those words were more powerful than any I had ever read.

I read Prévert's poem that begins, "Remember Barbara/It rained all day on Brest that day/And you were walking radiant/Rushing ravishing rippling/In the rain/ Remember Barbara."

I remember being deeply moved in those chilly classrooms. A woman with white hair in a tight bun and the passion for words that was like a constant euphoria that she moved in, the euphoria of the French intellectual, taught us Surrealist poems that changed my life, made me concentrate all my studies on literature from then on. She read us the poem of Paul Éluard that begins, *Jours de lenteur, jours de pluie.*

Those were my days. Days of slowness, days of rain. The winter came, in darkness and colder rain, and my hours spent reading in my unheated room became distinctly tough. I would read in my coat and hat.

I was lonely; I missed my capricious Canadian girlfriend (who had taken to writing me hurtful letters) with an intensity that only an

53

18-year-old can experience. I longed for Canadian comfort. I listened obsessively to the BBC on my tiny transistor radio, my lifeline to a familiar culture. I even used to listen to the British weather reports. They were somehow consoling.

It's hard to remember what life was like before e-mail and VCRs. In the evenings, without a phone, I wrote letters by hand. This didn't bother me; few French students had phones. I felt no need for one. Nor was I then even used to watching television; I didn't miss it or ever think about it. My sole entertainment, when alone, was words. And I have never been so focused, so intelligent. Words became concrete to me, magical objects that burned and glowed in my mind. I could read 17th-century classical drama for hours, something I would have to force myself to do now. It was so real to me I would cry at Racine – another talent I have probably lost. *Jours de lenteur, jours de pluie.*

One of the writers I discovered that year was the poet Apollinaire, who wrote, "People don't leave anything without regret; even the places, the things and the people that have made them unhappiest they cannot abandon without pain." And now I miss that melancholy grey room with the high ceiling and the loaf of bread and my socks drying on a rack, and the window onto the rain, and recognize it as the most fertile room of my life.

54

Time Honoured

MARNI JACKSON LOOKS FORWARD TO ANOTHER COSY
CHRISTMAS AT HOME.

Home, to my husband and 16-year-old son, is a Toronto semi with damn few comfortable chairs, some art on the walls, and a backyard with a garden teetering on the brink of chaos. The thing I like about it, though, is the view out the sliding doors over the invisible subway sleeper yard behind us — a prairie of sky that's hard to come by in the city. The only problem is, our house is too small for an extended family Christmas. So, with any luck, the 12 of us will assemble, one more time, at my parents' home in Burlington, Ontario. My mother is 89 and my father is 91, so dinner may be scaled back a little. But I'm sure we can count on more than one sort of cranberry relish.

To me, home still means my parents' place, where I spent my high school years (mostly in front of the upstairs bathroom mirror). The house is a cream-coloured three-bedroom bungalow on a corner lot with spruce trees, front and back. I remember the trees as runts, but now they tower over the house.

In Toronto, our unfinished basement is for storage, and laundry. But my parents' home has the classic '50s rec room: wet bar, TV, ping-pong table, non-regulation pool table, and what used to be called a "fruit cellar" (which would now be used for wine). My mother's ceramic kiln is still down there too, along with the clay figures she has sculpted over the years. She keeps these figures in the fruit cellar, and over the years some of them have been sprayed gold and pressed into service as Christmas angels.

Rec rooms come in handy for working off Christmas dinners. Every year, after we've eaten way too much, the grandchildren (all boys) will drift downstairs to play pool, or yet another game of air hockey. The adults will lie about the living room in a semi-invalid state, digesting, and reading the instructions to the small appliances we have just unwrapped. Around this time, I will notice one big difference between our urban house, where computers have invaded two bedrooms, and my parents' home. They may not buy rice-paper lamps, but they do understand comfort. Their house, by no means lavish, has three couches, all of them more nap-worthy than our trendy leather number. Our place has antique wooden chairs. My parents' home, on the other hand, has a brace of cushy upholstered chairs that rock, swivel, tilt and recline. These chairs can snap you upright, or grip you deep in their upholstered wings. They have little cups under the feet, to protect the rug. Close at hand are hassocks on wheels, shawls, neck pillows for better views of the TV, pencils for note-taking, baskets of reading matter to accessorize bad sitcoms, small dishes for roasted peanuts and trivets for tea. My parents have raised the business of sitting in an armchair to an art.

57

When I asked my son what he remembers from early Christmases at his grandparents', he thought for a minute and said, "Crawling around on the rug." Alas, he won't have many rug memories of our house. We went the urban, allergy-free route — hardwood floors and kilims. No rolling on the broadloom with the family dog for him. We do have a ping-pong table, but it's folded up behind all the Mountain Equipment Co-op gear in the basement. No, for a homey home, he has to visit his grandparents' home, where everything is thickly padded — not just the broadloom, but the dining-room table, the ironing board, and the lawn furniture too. My parents grew up in hard-working families in the Prairies. They married during the Depression, made their way east, and raised three kids. The refuge of a comfortable, safe home, equipped with "labour-saving devices," is something they never take for granted.

So home to me means comfort, and food — my mother's wonderful and ingenious cooking, my father's careful oiling of all the house's moving parts. Their clothes dryer has lasted more than 30 years because, as my father says, "all it needs is a drop of oil every time you use it, and it works perfectly." My mother approaches cooking as both an art and a science (she majored in Household Science in university). She loves food, and has studied nutrition all her life; my father's vitality at the age of 91 bears out her theories. Pleasure comes first. Chocolate is one of the major food groups. There may be Vitamin E on the counter, but there is always ice cream in the freezer.

For most families, Christmas is about tradition, but my mother is always experimenting with food. She served jicama in salads before I knew how to spell it, and she was tossing nasturtiums into salads back when Martha Stewart was still figuring out how to fold napkins into little crowns. Our family is full of delicate eaters on various regimes — anti-gout, no-chicken, dairy shunners, vegetarians — all the things that drive

good cooks crazy. This just ups the ante for my mother, and she finesses these culinary challenges like a rock climber finding a route around a ledge. I think we had Christmas without a turkey once too, but sooner or later turkey always creeps back on the menu. (We stopped short of ordering "tofurkey," the all-tofu vegetarian turkey.)

Christmas at my parents' home is always casual, but there is a subtle choreography involved. First come The Dips — many, many appetizers, deployed on the long coffee table in the living room. My mother is the queen of dips, ranging from the classic '50s mayonnaise combos to fashionable sweet-potato purées or roasted eggplant concoctions with little shovels of endive. "Try this," she will say, steering us over to the coffee table. "It's mostly roasted red peppers with just a bit of cream cheese." Baby aubergines, turkey bacon, tomatillos, star fruit — if it has been okayed by the Food and Drug Act, my mother will have used it at least once.

Christmas dinner will also include our own contributions — my sister-in-law's fabulous homemade truffles, my brother-in-law's Waldorf salad. My husband and I will bring the wine, and maybe some slightly tortured vegetable dish out of *Gourmet* magazine. By popular demand, my mother-in-law will come bearing her turnip puff — a divine dish that uses mashed turnip to deliver as much cream, eggs and butter to the table as possible. My mother will have risen early to manhandle the turkey off the counter and into the oven. We will open the door and peer at it often, like a preemie in an incubator. Even though we have made my mother promise to "only do the turkey," she may then "just make a casserole or two," usually involving 8 or 10 ingredients, possibly water chestnuts.

Around 4:30, the activity in the kitchen will accelerate. The smoke alarm in the kitchen hall will go off, as it always does. Someone will shut it off with the broomstick, and my mother will check to make sure

Sooner or later one of us will say something that makes us all stop eating and laugh, in a genuine, helpless way. It may be the sort of joke that only the 12 of us could ever understand.

something on the stove isn't burning. Quite possibly, something is burning. Babying risotto for 20 minutes is not her forte — she likes to crank up the heat and get those carrots cooked. Both my sister and I have inherited the burning-pot syndrome. I tend to burn steamers — the water underneath always evaporates when I'm on the phone or downstairs checking for mildew in the laundry. My artist sister is an insouciant pot-burner; her husband likes to tell stories about how they can look out the kitchen window after the snow melts in spring and see the pots that were tossed, smoking, out the back door over the winter.

Although my mother hates to repeat recipes, certain traditions around Christmas have accumulated over the years. The pine cone place cards that my sister-in-law made will be unpacked and deployed around the table. My sister made a miniature Christmas tree, perfect right down to the tiny skis and ski poles underneath, and that will go on the table too. My husband, deprived of a barbecue, will undertake the masculine chore of uncorking the wine, and possibly carving the turkey too. Everyone will be slightly narcotized by a round of pre-dinner manhattans.

Then we'll sit down at the long, linen-covered table, with the turkey down at my father's end, and the vegetables in silver serving dishes at my mother's. Plates of food will circulate up and down. There will, in fact,

60

be two sorts of relish — orange-cranberry, and the ordinary kind. My brother and I at this point may strike up a spirited conversation about gallstones or Crohn's disease, and my sister's husband, a normal person from P.E.I., will then make a joke about the typical Jackson dinner-table topic being wound drainage or something equally repellent. My father may propose a witty and slightly sentimental toast. Daniel, his youngest grandson, will eat only truffles and buns. Then he will slide off his chair and go "crawling on the rug" the way my son used to. As the plates go round, we will all heap a volcano of food on the one that goes to Jacob — male, 27, and thin, he is the Designated Diner.

My father will then either turn his hearing aid up or down, depending on what is being said. Several desserts will appear, and my mother will remind everyone that there is "nothing in them." Someone will point out that one of the fat-free cakes appears to be drenched in chocolate, but it's "dark chocolate, 70 per cent cocoa," my mother will say, "so it's fine."

It won't all be jolly. Christmas never is. Christmas marks time in sad and unavoidable ways. But sooner or later one of us will say something that makes us all stop eating and laugh, in a genuine, helpless way. It may be the sort of joke that only the 12 of us could ever understand. And we'll be grateful for one more dinner together, in the house we still call home.

Home Improvement

KATE FILLION FINDS THAT HOUSE-HUNTING OFFERS UNIQUE
OPPORTUNITIES TO REINVENT HERSELF.

Three years ago, we moved from Toronto to rural Pennsylvania,
primarily because I fell in love with a very large and quite formal 250-year-
old house. It wasn't an obvious choice for a childless couple who could
barely fix a leaky faucet, but I didn't want to change the house. I wanted it
to change us, to make us more capable yet also more elegant.

Believing that a house can confer a new identity is a common
delusion. I recently met a woman who confessed that she bought her
home largely because it had a window seat, and she imagined that with
a window seat, she'd become a reader. "I saw myself getting through
War and Peace and actually liking it," she said dreamily, then added,
"I don't think I've ever sat there for more than a minute or two. It was the
idea of it I liked."

62

I knew just what she meant. I had liked the idea of living in a very old house, but it hadn't occurred to me that very old floors don't take kindly to shoes, dogs or anything else that moves, with the possible exception of a mop. After a while, the exquisitely wrought chair rails got on my nerves too: their main purpose appeared to be to collect dust. And sometimes, something would go so weirdly wrong that I'd have no idea whether to call a plumber, stonemason or general contractor. Predictably, we still couldn't fix anything ourselves.

By last winter, I was surreptitiously reading real estate ads and imagining how much better life would be if only we lived somewhere else. Then, one day in March, I happened to walk into the post office at the precise moment that Eileen, the postmistress, was telling someone that a woman I'll call Jane had decided to sell her house. Around here everyone knows, or at least knows of, everyone else, but I'd never heard of Jane. And yet she lived less than a mile from us, in a house tucked back in the woods. It was old yet completely renovated, and boasted an addition that Eileen deemed "spectacular." Oh, and there was a huge barn, a pond and 40 acres of rolling meadows. By the time I got home, I was ready to bid on Jane's house, sight unseen. She had land, whereas we had 5 measly acres. She had radiant heat; we had windows seemingly designed to conduct cold air into the house.

Within 48 hours, I'd convinced my husband that we ought to at least see Jane's house. "It never hurts to look," I told him as we pulled into her driveway. I'd found out a little more about her in the meantime, namely that her business was in a bit of financial trouble, which was why she was selling her home. But when she answered the door, she looked serene, and the house smelled of something baking, something with cinnamon and cloves.

Really, it was more cottage than house, but the kitchen was a showplace: miles of counter space and state-of-the-art appliances. My husband

was equally taken with the property, which provided a stunning view of the valley. A reel of the future unspooled in my head: him, riding by the window on a tractor, while I calmly baked a cinnamon-and-clove thing. Yes, if we lived here, we would be different people, people who were competent and unflappable, much like, say, Jane.

She interrupted my reverie to say she wanted to sell the house privately — no realtors — and quickly. She was not much past 30, and had the confidence that comes from early success. Even besotted with the kitchen as I was, I was dimly aware that I didn't just want her house. I wanted her life.

Five days later, during which time our mothers inquired repeatedly whether we'd lost our minds, we told Jane we'd buy her house. "It was fate," she and I burbled at each other. She hadn't even had to advertise! And we'd found the perfect house simply by going to the post office! Really, we agreed smugly, this was the perfect illustration of the difference between living in the city, where everything was so difficult, and living in the country, where you could seal a deal with a handshake. Eileen was thrilled for everyone — including herself, after Jane presented her with a lavish gift.

It did seem like fate, especially after John, our realtor and close friend, sold our house in two days to a couple from Seattle, who made a full-price cash offer. When I called Jane to share the news, she sounded almost as excited as I was, and told me to drop by the next day to pick up the signed agreement of sale for her house.

If you haven't yet guessed what happened next, perhaps you can understand why we were stunned when Jane announced, two hours after we'd blithely signed away our own home, that, regrettably, she was legally unable to sell her house. It was entangled in her business affairs and, as became clear after three miserable weeks, she could not even sign something saying she would like to sell it to us.

64

Yet we didn't really face the fact that we were about to be homeless until the day Jane hired a new lawyer who instructed us not to call his client again, "because she's under a great deal of stress." Our own lawyer informed us that the couple from Seattle would sue if we tried to back out of our deal with them, and advised us to begin house-hunting immediately.

As we soon discovered, there was nothing for sale in our township. The prospect of losing our neighbourhood was even more distressing to my husband than the prospect of losing our house, and it was at this point, if memory serves, that he more or less stopped speaking to me.

I couldn't blame him. In fact, the only person I loathed more than myself was Jane. Yes, it had been idiotic to take her at her word, but at least I'd been honourably idiotic. Jane, on the other hand… It got so that I couldn't even say her name without sputtering.

I insisted that John show us every house in a 20-mile radius, no matter how unsuitable. We actually bid on one dreary handyman's special, then withdrew our offer at the eleventh hour, when it looked as though it might be accepted. We knocked on the doors of houses we liked, asking the owners if they had ever considered selling. Or renting. My husband was distraught, but after a while I realized I was enjoying myself: with each new house we saw came a potential new life. I didn't want to stop looking, because it would mean choosing just one vision of the future… and one version of myself.

The day we finally found a rental, Jane's lawyer called: she had cleared away the legal obstacles and was now able to sign an agreement of sale, though we would have to close immediately. By this point, however, I was smitten with the rental property, which had the most wonderful fireplace: "I can see myself in the winter, knitting in front of a roaring fire…" My husband didn't wait to hear the rest, nor did he point out that I don't know how to knit. He was already on his way to Jane's house to get her signature.

65

While he was gone, I began to panic: now that I had exactly what I'd said I wanted, I was no longer certain that I wanted it. I'd betrayed our beautiful home, where we'd been very happy, for what? A flashy kitchen? A week later, sitting in Jane's kitchen while the home inspector nosed around, I felt positively queasy. Why hadn't I noticed before how small and pokey the house was? And how on earth could we ever take care of 40 overgrown acres? I was secretly delighted when the inspector announced grimly that the septic system was shot and the electrical service to the house had never been completed. My husband, however, was furious — especially after Jane refused to lower her asking price. But we weren't exactly in a strong negotiating position: we had to move in three weeks and had no other options. Someone else had snapped up the rental.

John called to commiserate, then mentioned that there were two new listings in our area. We raced out to see them, but they were dismal horrors. Then, because we were desperate, we finally let him drag us to a place we had always refused to see because it was everything we were certain we didn't want: a huge house on a small piece of land far south of where we wanted to live. We hated the sound of it, but when we saw it we couldn't resist the eight-foot-high windows or the endless second-floor balcony. The house was like a mirror in which we could see ourselves clearly, not as we would like to be but as we actually are: the kind of people who sip cool drinks on the porch while a contractor rips out the kitchen.

We made an offer the next day and moved in this past summer. We're very happy, especially when we think of our phantom selves, stuck in our old house, or Jane's house, or the rental property. We liked the idea of those places, but here we like the reality. It feels like home, give or take a kitchen.

66

NOTES FROM ANTIQUES
Home Improvement
KATE FILLION

First Houses

BONNIE BURNARD RECALLS THE HOMES OF HER YOUTH.

When I was very young, before I could read on my own, the story I chose above all others to have read to me was about a little girl who had her own playhouse. The book had a soft cover with a small corner tear and on the front a black-and-white spaniel, and something red, perhaps the words of the title, which I have forgotten. In the illustrations, at least in my memory of the illustrations, the girl wore bright green cotton shorts, a blouse, and white ankle socks with black, strapped shoes, and she had at hand several household implements to help her make this small, rough space a home, among them a miniature tea set and a girl-sized broom. I remember her sweeping especially, and the seriousness with which she swept. She was a devoted, fastidious housekeeper, that little girl. Of course, I imagined myself in the playhouse wielding that broom, making that tea and, although she did sometimes entertain a few friends,

68

and quite well, I'm sure now that it wasn't the sweeping or the tea that caught my fancy but the independence, the self-sufficiency, the privacy.

I remember other houses too. In my first year at school there was a pretty little house at the back of the room, behind our rows of desks, which probably had been commissioned by our teacher, the tiny, grey-haired Miss O'Brien, and built by a pair of fathers who could not refuse her soft-spoken request. At the crest of its dark, steeply pitched roof, the house would have been about six feet high. It had been built most certainly with flimsy plywood, but at six I didn't know the difference between plywood and mahogany, so to me it looked like any house should look, with good solid walls painted white and pastel trim around the door and the windows. Inside, there were real cotton curtains that could be closed and several storybooks piled on a small painted bench. It was Miss O'Brien's rule that if you finished your desk work quickly and properly, you could go into the house to read. I didn't always get there first but I worked as hard and fast as I could, all for the promise of privacy. This was my first taste of privacy as reward, and I can remember the sensation of curling up on that bench as easily as I can remember sitting at my own breakfast nook an hour ago, eating a leftover spring roll for lunch as I opened the mail.

But I must have been drawn by something more than privacy because there were shared houses too. There was the community of play, or the playing at community. The seasons helped. In the fall, sent out to rake maple and chestnut leaves, to haul them to the street to burn at the curb, the burning supervised by my mother or one of my older brothers and the pungent smell of the burning heavy in the cool October air, my friends and I raked floor plans. All the rooms had low leaf walls and green grass floors and, because our house, our real house, was on a double lot with a wide breadth of open yard, the rooms could be huge, sometimes

69

much bigger than life-sized. There had to be a living room, of course, and a kitchen and dining room, and these had to be connected by hallways as they would be in any sensible house, and then there were bedrooms to add at the back, and a bathroom. Occasionally, there would be a library or a maid's room or a nursery, because we knew there were people whose lives required such rooms and, who knew, we might someday be among them. The walls would shift a bit in a breeze but they were easily straightened with a rake. Real wind was never a worry because my mother did not burn leaves on windy days. Boys who wandered the streets looking for some-thing to do, the boys who sat behind us at school distracting us with jokes or plaguing us with small, often original, cruelties, would sometimes come tearing through the gate to kick through our delicate walls, but this was anticipated. We understood those boys. We had given them careful thought because they were the boys we had crushes on, the ones who always came to temptation on the run. They didn't surprise us.

We made floor plans at the beach too, using long thin sticks of drift-wood to mark our rooms in the perfect stretch of sand between the soft, drifting dune sand and the wave-wet shoreline. People walking the beach in their bathing suits often paid us the courtesy of skirting our property, asking: Is that the living room, with the two fireplaces? Or: Do you think you need so many doors?

In those summers, there were always blankets thrown over someone's clothesline and stretched wide at the base to make a tent, the frayed satin blanket edges held down with bricks carried from a pile behind some garage. Dolls were brought into this shelter, and plastic guns and games of snakes and ladders, and flashlights and magazines with pictures of shameless women in black underwear. The Freshie got spilled on the quilts that made our floor, and some quite disgusting insects found the salmon sandwiches and the hermit cookies, and once, in the middle of a sleepless,

In those summers, there were always
blankets thrown over someone's clothesline
and stretched wide at the base to make
a tent, the frayed satin blanket edges held
down with bricks carried from a pile
behind some garage.

giddy night, there was a raccoon. The least bit of excitement could and
did ruin these houses, but never beyond repair.

One winter, which the adults would have called a bad winter because
there had been unusual and relentless snowfall, the boys at the end of
our street built a snow house. Perhaps it began as a straightforward igloo,
as warmth and shelter from an imagined storm, but soon there were
arches leading to rooms and a back door and hard-packed seats to sit on
and ledges to hold things. I don't remember what leverage we used to
get inside, what skills or gifts we offered, but we did get inside. We did
crawl from room to room, careful not to break the snow.

There was the big, wired crate that brought my mother's first dishwasher, a top-loading technological wonder that was attached to a sink
with stainless steel drainboards and, like many of the other technological
wonders in that kitchen, used sparingly because my mother remained
convinced until she died that sometimes it was easier, and certainly quicker,
just to push up your sleeves and do the thing yourself. The emptied crate
was put in the basement for my pleasure. I suspect I begged for it. The door
was hinged with wires but it was very hard to close because they had been

careless when they pried it open to get at the dishwasher. The slats of wood were pale and raw, which meant splinters in a moment of carelessness.

At my cousins' farm the strongest boys stacked bales of hay to make connecting rooms. There were tunnels between the rooms and carefully engineered windows. There were hay-bale chairs and hay-bale steps leading up to a second and sometimes a third storey, and sometimes a window in the roof, a skylight. The barn cats prowled the rafters, hating the disturbance we were, and small birds taunted them, perching for only seconds and then bursting out through the wide-open doors to the summer sky, to the fields.

Later, there were cottages. In the three or four summers before we separated for university or marriage or jobs, 5 of us, or 8, or 10, it scarcely mattered, rented a cottage on the shores of Lake Huron. Our parents, who had always been with us at cottages, didn't inquire about any of the details and they were far too smart to drop in unannounced. We brought our own bedding and food and someone's new stereo. The sagging mattresses were thin and the fireplaces sometimes didn't draw well. The kitchens were primitive, but all we really needed to keep us going was a bowl of cereal or ice cream. Spaghetti could be managed. Spaghetti was big in 1963, spaghetti and red wine, which was always Chianti because of the bottles with the baskets, for candles. The guys bought the beer and drank most of it. People got sunburned. People threw up. A few times someone who couldn't stand it any longer would clean up the kitchen or sweep the gritty sand out the door, but most of the time most of us didn't care. It's the stars I remember, their sheen on the water. The stars and pulling on a cold, clammy bathing suit for a late-night swim, one more swim under those stars.

Soon there were serious apartments, either the upstairs of an old brick house or a three-bedroom spread in a brand new high-rise. Derelict sofas were borrowed. Parents' basements were raided for bookcases and lamps and curtain rods. There were aqua dishes made from something previously unknown to mankind, so tough they could be dropped without a second thought. Curtains were matched to cushions, and there were useful, thoughtful gifts: a set of mixing bowls, thick American towels, a pair of heavy down pillows, a radio, all of it valued as never before, all of it long since given away, misplaced, left behind.

Like other lucky people, I have since that time enjoyed the luxury of a proper, private home, four of them in 27 years: the first a modest bunga-low built when we were first married; the second a big old two-storey that will always be the house the kids mean when they say the word "home"; the third a brand new empty-nester; the last this spread-out ranch with beautiful trees and too much yard. And each of these houses were antici-pated, their shelter dreamed so early in my life, those dreams now turned to memory – of a hollering, laughing boy kicking through a wall of leaves, or the song of birds on the rafters of a summer barn, or the watching from the safety of a screened-in porch as roaring, ruinous storm waves washed our plans away, the churning waves oblivious to our disappointment and equally unaware that we were young, with the whole, sun-baked summer at our feet.

73

Near Perfect

DAVID MACFARLANE RECALLS THE UNEASY BEGINNINGS AND
EVOLVING PLEASURES OF A CHERISHED SUMMER TRADITION.

Being a guest isn't the easiest thing in the world.
Particularly a guest at a summer cottage. My memories of weekends at one
friend's cottage when I was young and cottageless — as opposed, I might
as well point out, to my current state of being middle-aged and cottageless
— involve lying uncomfortably in bed in the early morning, a nervous
wreck, ears attuned to every creaking floorboard, trying to decide whether
the coast was clear to get to the one bathroom without greatly inconve-
niencing my hosts. Once in the bathroom, time was of the essence, of
course, but there was also the additional stress of trying to go about one's
business as silently as possible, since all the walls were made of something
called beaverboard — a soft, brown substance that gloomily absorbed
light but that seemed to take a certain glee in amplifying sound. This was

in the days when cottages were cottages — not monster homes plunked down on the side of a lake — and plumbing was quaintly idiosyncratic. In my memory, my nervous, 45-second morning visits to the bathroom always ended with me staring in horror at the sluggish and slowly rising whirlpool of a toilet that resolutely declined to flush, while outside the bathroom door Mrs. Ward was gently wondering if anyone was in there.

It got worse. As a visitor to a cottage, I was reminded constantly of my status as a non-cottager. This had nothing to do with any ungraciousness or snobbery on my hosts' part. The Wards couldn't have been more friendly or generous. It's just that there were ways of doing things at cottages — of inserting an empty Rice Krispies box into the wood stove without burning down the island; of tying up a boat so that, should the need ever arise, it might someday be untied — that were not perfectly obvious to the uninitiated. My friend's father was a great handyman, a characteristic that was notable in the city but that, in the realm of the cottage, he seemed to upgrade from hobby to religion. Mr. Ward and his alarmingly organized shed full of tools were devoted to halting the natural devolution to decrepitude of shutters, roofs, docks. As a result, the care of these inanimate objects was transformed into summer pastimes called chores. And, naturally, part of my role as a guest was to help with these chores. There were times — creosoting the bunkie springs to mind — when I wondered whether Mr. Ward was of the conviction that it was my only role. But there was something about my unfamiliarity with the cottage — to say nothing of the fact that in our household no one could ever find my father's one tool, a badly rusted hammer — that made everything seem hopelessly complicated. Mr. Ward's most simple requests — "Fetch me the Number three Robertson, would you, Dave" or "Pass me the crosscut saw" — would paralyze me completely. People often have dreams of being onstage without knowing the lines of the play they are

supposed to be in. To this day my nightmares involve being a guest. I am back at the Wards' cottage, and Mr. Ward is asking me to undertake certain cottagey tasks of which I haven't a clue: put the cover on the boat; tie a bowline; trim the wicks; raise the flag — properly; drain the sump.

These were the thoughts that passed through my mind eight years ago when my wife announced that we had been invited to a summer cottage in Temagami for a week. Oh great, I thought, picturing myself toeless and waist-deep in freezing water, heaving boulders into my host's newly repaired crib; frying on a roof while saying cheerfully, "Oh, no. There's no skin cancer in our family, and, anyway, shingling has always been something I've enjoyed"; trying to get to sleep while six inches from my head, through walls that might as well be paper, the resident insomniacs sit up until 3 a.m. playing a few quiet games of poker and what sounds like touch football; listening to the howling north wind, and the hail, and the sound of trees being uprooted, and the sputter of damp, smoky firewood, while the cottage-owners distribute blankets and apologetically explain that in all their summers they've never seen weather quite like this.

My first question, which my wife thought distinctly odd, was how many bathrooms do they have.

I'll call them Lorraine and Philip, for they might be embarrassed by any undue attention. And the fact was we didn't know them all that well back then. My wife and I had worked on a book project for this magazine with Lorraine, and had come to like her enormously. I managed to miss every deadline she gave me, but Lorraine, who was developing a firm friendship with my wife, inexplicably appeared to enjoy my company as well. We had been invited to their home for dinner, and had met Philip, who turned out to be congenial and gracious and funny. We were introduced to their two young daughters. I'll call them Aly and Meredith. Even then, when the girls were little more than toddlers, I found myself feeling sorry for the boys whose teenage hearts they were bound to break a few years hence. The dinner had been a success, and I was looking forward to seeing more of Lorraine and Philip. But, still… A week at a cottage — with our kids. This was an unexpected upping of our relationship. I was familiar enough with cottage life to know that there are not so many weeks in a Canadian summer that cottagers can offer them around willy-nilly. Obviously, a good deal of thought had gone into an invitation that filled me with both anticipation and cottagey dread.

I can't go into any details of the evolution from pre-arrival anxiety to the pleasure of being at Lorraine and Philip's cottage, for the simple reason that there weren't any. We were made to feel at home at once, which — after an eight-hour drive with young children — was accomplished by our attentive host adding freshly squeezed orange juice and ice to a healthy wallop of vodka. If being a guest isn't the easiest thing in the world, being a host is no picnic either. Who knows what deformities of character will be revealed when people are transported from the comforts of the city to a remote boathouse dock?

A remote boathouse dock on which we, the unpredictable guests, had stood gaping over the peaks of our immodest cordillera of luggage. Gaping at the trees, the rock, the water, the paths, the sky. To my shame, I'd never been to Temagami before. And obviously we had landed at what was a very, very beautiful place. Philip had seemed undismayed by the fact that it looked as if we had packed enough clothes for a month and enough food for an army. Everyone pitched in; our things were lugged up to our cabins, our supplies were deposited in the kitchen. Which was when Philip took accurate stock of the situation and said, "You look like you need a drink."

You may have noticed that I said "cabins" — and it was this plural that was the first, and the biggest, clue that we had arrived at a place that

> I have to admit that my first apprehension of delight came when I realized that there were sleeping cabins. Separate sleeping cabins, all well away from one another, and well away from the central cottage!

approached perfection. Temagami is beautiful; the tall-pined island is beautiful; the view from the Adirondack chairs at the front of the cottage is beautiful; the quiet, lily-padded bay at the back of the island is beautiful. Early on, Philip made it perfectly clear that chores were not going to be part of my cottage agenda — and I considered this news quite beautiful. But I have to admit that my first apprehension of delight came when I realized that there were sleeping cabins. Separate sleeping cabins, all well away from one another, and well away from the central cottage! Our kids would be in one; our hosts in another; and we'd be in another. Suddenly — for the thought had never crossed my mind — I came to understand that we would actually get some rest at a cottage.

The main cottage, built by Philip's father, is a simple log structure, consisting basically of a dining area, a living room area, a screened porch, a kitchen, and two small rooms at the back of the cottage used for storage and for the kids' art room. I say simple, which it is, but its simplicity is of the best kind: unassuming, perfectly functional, and (the hackneyed term always seems to brush away its overuse when I look at our summer snapshots) as pretty as a picture. With its weathered logs, shadowy shingles, and modest size, the cottage, nestled among the majestically tall pines, is almost invisible from the water.

78

All daily activity centres on the main cottage: the long shifts of poached eggs and malt toast and sausages; the coffee and books and two-day-old newspapers in front of the fire; the kids drawing and painting and sculpting in the art room; the dough-kneading and bread-rising in the kitchen; the heated grudge-matches of badminton in the little clearing outside the kitchen door; the late dinners when we sit by candlelight and drink wine and retell old stories and agree that whatever dreadful flaws Martha Stewart may possess, her recipe for blueberry pie — berries picked by Philip and me and the children, the pie baked by Lorraine — is the best any of us has ever tasted.

That's the main cottage. But the genius of this lovely spot is that sleeping, etc., is done in several small cabins that are tucked away in the Temagami woods. And it's this arrangement that establishes the perfect balance of communal and private living that is the hallmark of Philip and Lorraine's summer place. You can play badminton with everyone, if you want. You can swim with everyone, if you want. You can sit in front of the main cottage and read with everyone, if you want. But, if you also want, you can go and read, undisturbed, in bed. You can go have a nap. You can sleep in. You can retire early. You can — well, there are any number of things you can get up to in a sleeping cabin when you're on a summer holiday. Peace, quiet, privacy, and schedules of sleeping and waking that are our own. You can keep your microwaves and saunas — this is real cottage luxury.

So, the invitation that had filled me with such initial anxiety turned out to be one of the best things to happen to us. Our hosts were as welcoming, as friendly, as easygoing, and as down-to-earth as the place where they spend their summers. We felt lucky to be there and, after our week, sad to leave. And then, somehow, we were asked back the next year. And then asked back again, and again, and again. And somehow —

magically, really — an unexpected invitation for a week at a cottage one summer has evolved into a cherished friendship and a much-loved tradition of two families: of sleep-outs at the boathouse, and picnics at High Rock, and kiddy talent shows, of screwdrivers (the chore-free variety), badminton, and swims around the island in the late afternoon, and stargazing on the clear, loon-calling nights. What was once a strange, unfamiliar place is now an irreplaceable part of our summer memories. I can, without effort, imagine the sound of the latch on the kitchen door, of the juicer preparing the oranges for cocktails, of the splashing and shouts of children at the red dock, of dogs barking when the launch, with Philip at the helm, comes rumbling around the point. It almost seems too much. And so, every year we say that they must not feel obligated, that we would understand, that they must not feel that they are stuck with us forever as guests. But every year this kind and impossibly generous invitation, like summer itself, is extended once more.

NOTES FROM HOME

DAVID MACFARLANE

Near Perfect

The View from There

CATHERINE BUSH LOOKS AT THE IMPACT OF CITY AND COUNTRY ON THE PLACES SHE HAS CALLED HOME.

Two contradictory desires tug at me: the urge to nest and the urge to roam. Over the last 16 years, the span of my adult life, I've lived in eight homes in four cities in two countries, plus shorter stints in sublets and house-sits. I've moved from two white rooms in New York City to a white room on Cape Cod, from a west-end Toronto house to an east-end Montreal apartment. I've slipped away to an antique-filled row house just off Camden High Street in London. Yet I'm not really much of a traveller; the idea of journeying from point A to B to C doesn't seduce me, even if A is Venice and C is Milan. What I fall for are places — rooms or cities — in which I can create, or temporarily improvise — a sense of home.

Some people find New York City huge and unfriendly. No one ever looks you in the eye there, a former boyfriend once said. This puzzled me, for my experience in New York has always been the opposite. In the street or on the subway, I often trade gazes with others. Random conversations start up. Perhaps, in part, what you expect from a place determines what it returns to you. And luck and chance encounters played a big role in my life in New York.

Just out of my American college, I applied for a summer job back at home in Toronto, which I didn't get, and angled for a furnished sublet in New York's Little Italy, which came through. Arriving by bus from Newark airport, I began talking to a man who told me he ran an alternative performance space in the East Village, who went on to introduce me to a community — a great extended family — of artists, including a man who invited me to write for the downtown paper he worked for and gave me the name of his landlord on Ludlow Street, where, when my sublet ended, I found my own apartment.

When I think of my home in New York, I think of this Lower East Side apartment, the first of two in the same building. Twin white, high-ceilinged rooms with a true bathroom, not, as in so many of those unrenovated tenement apartments, a bathtub in the kitchen. In the black-and-white tiled kitchen sat the bright pink stove bequeathed to me by the woman who lived there before me. I loved the pink stove so much that I took it with me when I moved to my second apartment, at the back of the same building, forced out of the first when a teenage son materialized in the midst of the Dominican family next door. Boombox cranked, he was the loudest thing on the block.

Both apartments shared another tenement rarity. Sky. Lots of it, great swaths filling the windows above the low roof of a warehouse and the flat tarmac of a parking lot. Some people want their homes to offer a sense of enclosure; I crave porousness. Give me sky and a glimpse of other people's lives. I take comfort in the propinquity of our jammed-together existences.

83

One fall, through the kitchen window of the Provincetown, Massachusetts, apartment where I lived for nine months, I watched a dead deer swing on the porch of the house next door, curing in all kinds of weather: wind and rain and sun. Down on the beach, the lobster fisherman who lived next door worked painstakingly, building traps of net and wood.

Through the windows of that apartment, the third floor of a shingled house, I had more sky than I knew what to do with, sky and water, the sun so bright some days across Cape Cod Bay that I had to wear sunglasses indoors. The view made up for the décor, a preponderance of blue floral patterns and the pride of the man who owned the house. I would have loved it better had the space been spare and raw, but it was a dream fulfilled to live in a house on the beach, and a fitting place to mourn my father's death from cancer months before. I found the rawness I needed in the weather, wind storms rattling the walls, a monster hurricane spitting seaweed as high as my third-storey windows.

When I moved back to Toronto, I virtually built a home, renovating the small house that a boyfriend and I shocked all our friends by buying six weeks after we got together as a couple. Time to settle, I told myself, and in Toronto, as in New York, I could live as I love to do, my sense of home rooted in my downtown neighbourhood, in the range of streets that I roam on foot, where I'm never surprised to bump into people I know. We took perverse pride in the skinniness of our house (eight feet at its narrowest point!) and reconstructed a kitchen in which the original structural support was a single stone column. When the relationship ended, I bought my partner out and remade the house again, as my own.

Oddly, Montreal is the city in which I've felt the least at home. Our responses to cities are, I think, almost chemical: we react to them as we do to people and sometimes, though it's the fault of neither party, the chemistry simply doesn't take. Others find Montreal romantic, exotic, but I felt displaced: it was not a city where I could claim or truly imagine a life.

A teaching job took me to Montreal not long after the break-up of that Toronto relationship. For two years, after renting out my beloved Toronto house, I lived on the Plateau, east of St. Denis, speaking functional French when I went shopping. I loved Montreal bagels. I hated the fluorescent gloom of the Métro. I was puzzled by the lack of birds in Mount Royal Park. Unmoored, I floated through the streets, my sense of home tied not to the city in which I lived but to my apartment. Perhaps this was why I searched more maniacally than I ever had for the perfect place to live: five white-walled rooms with scuffed pine floors and angel heads on the mouldings. Friends who visited told me the apartment was so beautiful I could never leave, though I knew I wouldn't stay from the moment I propped (and didn't hang) the folk-art angel I'd carried through every move on nails left in the walls by the couple who had lived there before me.

These days, settled back in my house in Toronto, I head to other cities for briefer visits, as a way to channel my inherent restlessness and playfully enter some alternative life. While I was working on a novel set in London, a friend found me a house-sit in Camden, far grander than anything my character could afford to live in, though I was happy to. Each morning I folded open the heavy wooden shutters in the living and dining rooms and closed them again after dusk. I lolled on the velvet-covered, horsehair-stuffed sofa. Each hour, the plethora of hand-wound clocks rang, each slightly out of sync with the other.

This past summer, I returned for a month to New York, subletting a sixth-floor East Village walk-up, blocks from where I used to live. This way, I could entertain the illusion of reentering my New York life.

Some people want their homes to offer a sense of enclosure; I crave porousness. Give me sky and a glimpse of other people's lives. I take comfort in the propinquity of our jammed-together existences.

I bought cut flowers at the Union Square greenmarket and, as I do in any city, headed out in search of unusual cheeses. I found a bar on Second Avenue to watch European soccer in. I hung hats on the walls: a form of portable art. Six floors up, the windows were full of sky and each morning I'd wake to watch the sun rise.

Whenever I leave my Toronto house, I feel agonized. In advance, I miss my tiny garden and the way the light falls across the walls of my study in the late afternoon. Once on the road, however, I'm fine. My true sense of home is portable. As long as I have light and a view, uncluttered walls and a couple of table surfaces to work on, I'm happy. And wherever I am, all my various homes are carried within me, winding their way through my internal landscape like a caravan.

86

Down Under

SHEILA HETI PONDERS HOW LIFE IN A BASEMENT APARTMENT
BOTH SPURRED AND THWARTED HER CREATIVITY.

Today I live in a third-floor apartment of an old
building with thin walls, and in the afternoons the light comes in so
beautifully I just want to bring people over and say, "Hey, look how the
light comes in so beautifully. Don't I live a happy life?" If I was ever to
move and saw an ad for a basement apartment I would not even look.
No sir. Not even if they said, "But madam! The light comes in just so!"
Never mind that. I like breezes and I love the sun but I like being inside
best, so I've got to be high up. I've got to have the outside inside.

But this story is not about breezes and sun. It is not about clean and
fresh apartments that make a gal feel free and alive. It is about basements.
I know a little something about basements because I was assaulted by the
twin fates that bring a young lady home to basements after having left her

88

parents a little too young and a little too proud: I broke up with my
boyfriend and, with him, our lovely grown-up red-walled apartment.

That is how I ended up in my mother's basement for a year, then my
father's basement for a year, before bounding three floors up to the light-
filled place I live in now, with the hardwood floors and the too-thin walls.

The room I moved into at my mother's was not like her other cool,
cluttered basement rooms. This one was the result of a renovation, and
that, plus her neatness, created a little oddly shaped white-walled room
with pink wall-to-wall carpeting and a windowed door to the backyard.
Off this room I even had my own bathroom. All of this was new enough
to be memory free, and, most promising of all, my mom was a busy
lady living three floors up. I practically had my own apartment again!

But this is not a story about the architecture of the room I took in
my mother's versus the architecture of the room I took at my father's, with
its low, practically domed white ceiling, wood-panelled walls and blood-
red rug, where I had the sense of being a smudge-faced stowaway in the
bottom of a ship. This is about how I wrote my first book of stories in the
basement of my mother's house, then the basement of my father's. I had
written nothing that went anywhere for the previous few years, only to be
strangely saved by the certain fertile power of basements. This is something I wouldn't normally claim, but it seems to have been the case.

Of course, to assume you wrote your book because you lived in one
basement after another is a kind of stupidity, not unlike wanting to drive
a bus when you've got a perfectly good bike, one that even children comment on. But there is something about basements that is just like the
middle of the night, and there is something about the middle of the night
that is just like being lost in space and time — which, when you're writing
fiction, certainly helps. Though now that I'm living in this nice, bright,
third-floor place with little breezes, I'd say there is also something about

Living in a basement apart from the world, where the seasons don't change and time doesn't pass, you get a good sort of vertiginous feeling of there being no consequence to anything you do.

working first thing in the morning that is like being lost – not in time and space quite, but in the middle of the sea.

When I moved home I didn't want to be lost in the middle of the sea. I had always written in the middle of the night and I needed to feel lost in that nighttime sort of way to work. Living in a basement, it's like night all the time. It makes it easy to feel like there's no world beyond your mud-enclosed walls. It makes it easy to believe you're the only person in town. These nighttime effects are very important, because if you're always thinking about how you offended this person or that, it's rather hard to write. And in a way, you need to forget a lot in order to write. Living under people's feet really does help with this. For instance, you forget that when you emerge from your cave you'll want to see a movie, but that you can't afford a movie, and how will you ever afford a movie again? Thinking all the time about how you'll afford a movie makes it quite hard to write.

Living in a basement apart from the world, where the seasons don't change and time doesn't pass, you get a good sort of vertiginous feeling of there being no consequence to anything you do. Turn on the light: it remains dark. Open the little window: it's still cool. Vacuum and dust: there's still dust. Burn a bit of incense: it still smells like basement.

Write an awful story: it almost never happened. Write a great story: no one's going to care. I recommend a basement for anyone who's doing work that will fail more often than not. In a basement, the failure's personal, minuscule. It has no connection to the outside world at all. A basement is the best place to fail: it's private, and besides, everything seems doomed in a basement. Life doesn't happen in basements; life happens in penthouses, in gardens, in swimming pools. A bad story written in a basement seems entirely appropriate. A bad story written in a villa in Nice is a significant blotch on the beauty of the world.

Before I moved back, I had worried about interruptions, about the persistent family stuff. But I soon learned that a basement is the essence of oblivion. No one knows what's in their basement. When people consider their basement, they think, I guess there's my old chess set down there. I might find a broken-down Commodore 64. Perhaps there are old movies; I just don't know. They think, I suppose if I searched I'd find my daughter. Do I have a daughter? What? It's not like living on the second floor. On the second floor you're the first thing a parent thinks of when there's dishes to be done. In the basement, well, it's hard to remember what you put there exactly.

There is, of course, a kind of madness to thinking and reading and writing and sleeping six feet below. It was in my father's basement that my fish died, and, paralyzed and bewildered, I left him there for half a week, disintegrating, as the whole room took on the smell of fish. It was at his place I began wandering around the first floor, without saying Hi or Hello Pa. "Stop this!" my father snapped, several times. "What is wrong with you?" It was at my mother's that one whole wall ended up covered with derisive quotations aimed at me, and, losing my keys all over the place, I began, like a rat, crawling into my room late at night through the tiny window which led to my desk.

At my father's, I wrote a story about a dumpling who fell under a kitchen table and lay there waiting to die, while the family who owned the house didn't even know there was a dumpling lying at their feet. "The dumpling's like you," my father said, "living in the basement." "Now, now," said I. "Let's please not talk about the stories that way." But indeed, the people in the fiction I wrote while living in the basement weren't quite part of the upstairs world. They were ugly people no one loved, and a widower who hadn't left his home in years, and a woman named Eleanor who lived with a family, but whose relation to them remained ambiguous. Naturally, it would be foolish to suggest that I wrote those stories simply because I was living in a basement rather than on a third floor — as foolish as wanting a bike when you have a beautiful Trans-Am. But there you go. That's just basement logic.

The combined effects of isolation and mania that basements foist onto a person made me feel weak and crazy the whole time, and not so dreamy as this upper-floor apartment does, with its swishy air and sunlight, and sense of bounce. So when I found out last week that I had to move home again, I remarked, after thoroughly considering a year of basement life, as a candid person must reply, "Ma'am, I'd rather stay in the sink."

Halloween Unmasked

DAVID EDDIE ON THE DAY THAT'S MORE FUN THAN CHRISTMAS.

"Dad, do you know what I want to be four Halloweens from now?"

"No."

"Guess."

"Dracula?"

"No, Dad," Nicholas said, becoming instantly angry, his eyebrows knitting low over eyes that are miniature replicas of his mother's, especially when angry. "That's what I want to be three Halloweens from now! What do I want to be four Halloweens from now?"

"I don't know."

"Guess!"

"A ... werewolf?"

94

A pause, during which I am on tenterhooks. I am so frightened of the wrath of my four-year-old child. I would do anything to avert it. Little beads of sweat form upon my brow.

"Yes! That's right, Dad. Good."

Phew.... No, there's very little doubt about it in my mind. Halloween is the high holiday of the child's calendar. Now, Christmas is a very competitive holiday, and naturally Nick looks forward to Christmas, sure. But he is looking forward to all the Halloweens of his life.

Halloween was always my favourite holiday, too. I was unable to give up trick-or-treating until well into my adolescence, when I was over six feet tall. I knew it was probably time to hang up the old cape (a beautiful old nursing cape of my mother's that I accessorized with stick-on fangs) when someone offered me a beer. That's when I knew it was time to quit. I think I did it for only another year after that.

It wasn't the candy. What I liked, and this may seem an odd thing to say in a magazine celebrating the pleasures of house and home, was that it was the only holiday that got you out of the house. Out into the streets. The other holidays are all about preparing the home, feathering the nest for an in-house execution of some cosy little ritual: finding some eggs, opening some presents. Halloween is about preparing yourself, donning some battle garb, and going out for an all-out assault on your neighbourhood and possibly points beyond. I liked that. It appealed to my rogue spirit, the side of the young David Eddie that craved adventure and action.

The other thing I liked about Halloween was it made no bones (joke) about what it was. Of the many confusing lies we tell our children surrounding Christmas, perhaps the most confusing is that we should pretend not to care about what presents we receive. That goes against fundamental human nature, at least as it manifests itself in the early stages. The thing

95

about children — in fact, I would go so far as to say one of the chief charms of children — is their transparency. Transparency and immediacy. Kids want what they want and they want it now — "Cookie! Cookie! Waaah!" — and any efforts they make to disguise what they want are charming and make you laugh. Because they're so obvious. And, of course, whenever they rise above the immediacy of their desires, when they spontaneously offer, say, a brother half a cookie, these moments are transcendent, because the parent knows the child is taking the first little step on a lifelong journey, a journey many do not complete in a lifetime, toward selflessness.

But think about being a kid. By a strange quirk of temperament, although I remember almost nothing of my childhood, I remember what it felt like to be a kid. I remember it as being very frustrating. Having to depend on two huge, slow-witted, heavy-footed, brontosaurus-like creatures to fulfill every little need. Brontosaurus-like creatures who said "yes" or "no" on what seemed like a capricious basis, who would say "no" to ice cream and "yes" to candy one day; then on the next reverse their positions! I could not wait until I grew up and had my own money — and I was right, it's better, even with all the worrying I do about it.

So I would posit that Christmas is about civilizing desire, sub-suming it, learning to pretend that the present isn't everything, swallowing cruel disappointment and kissing a withered cheek even when one feels one's spirit crushed by the failure of a certain present to appear. And this is good, this is necessary, this is what a child will need to grow up and take his/her place in polite society.

But Halloween is the necessary antidote to all that. On Halloween, we do not trouble to disguise our desires; it is ourselves we disguise. Naked greed prowls the streets. I recall on one of my first Halloweens as a hand-out-candy parent, I made the fatal mistake of offering kids the whole bowl

of candy. Whomp! Clomp! They came down on the bowl like little veloci-raptors, spiriting huge handfuls into their capacious bags (the smartest kids carry huge garbage bags now). I had to close up shop early that year, turn off the lights, put up a sign, and sit inside in fear and trembling of getting my windows soaped.

And if you have anything good to offer, you have to keep a sharp eye out for recidivists, those repeat "customers" who come back two, three, four times, in a naked attempt to beat the system.

"Hey," you think, like Hamlet, "where have I seen that ghost before?"

"Ha, ha! Sucker!" one (older) kid said to me last year when I finally figured out he had already been to the house (at least) once, and I told him to beat it. He did not have to add "Screw you, pops!" But I knew that's what he was thinking. And I like that kind of thing: naked greed, aggression, mixing it up with the neighbours. It's humanity in the raw, stripped of its cheap faux-mahogany veneer of civilization.

Of course, Christmas has its own insipid door-to-door tradition, too: carolling. My wife, Pam, finally convinced me to do that, last year. It was a nightmare. I will carry the memory of that humiliation to my grave. I still wake up in a sweat, sometimes, thinking about it.

We went around to our neighbours' houses, rang the doorbell, launched into "Good King Wenceslas," or what have you. A couple of neighbours were charmed. Most though, reacted with ill-concealed irritation — like Bridget Jones, who, in the movie, just opens her windows on a group of carollers and shouts an unprintable imprecation at them, then shuts the window. In the movie theatre when I saw it, everyone cheered.

It was like that. One woman who answered her door was on her phone. "Oh, um, it's some carollers," she said into the receiver. Merrily, we belted out "We Three Kings of Orient Are," or some such. She stayed on the phone the whole time. Sometimes, she muttered into it. When we finished our song, she nodded, smiled a tight little smile, and went back into her house.

I burn with shame even to recall that night. I prayed for some kind of costume. And that's one of the great beauties of Halloween, for me. You are not attempting to charm or please your neighbours, in any way. "Give me some candy or I soap your windows." I find it all very relaxingly natural and straightforward.

Halloween has been on the run a bit lately, which is a shame. It's had a lot of negative publicity. Nick's kindergarten teacher, for example, a staunch Christian, refuses even to allude to it. One grade-school teacher I know, a friend's mother, dressed up as a fortune-teller one Halloween, for fun, and received numerous complaints for promoting a "pagan" holiday.

Actually, while it is true that Halloween has certain influences that predate Christianity, mostly from Celtic rituals marking the beginning of winter, it is as Christian a holiday as Christmas. November 1 is All Saints Day, in which the Roman Catholic and Anglican churches glorify God for all his saints, known and unknown. It is one of the principal feasts of the year in the Roman Catholic Church. At one time, all were required to hear mass on it and observe a vigil of fasting and abstinence. It's also known as Allhallows and Hallowmass. The night before is All Hallows Eve. Trick-or-treating began with a ninth-century European custom called "souling." Early Christians would walk from village to village begging for "soul cakes," made out of square pieces of bread with currants. The more soul cakes they received, the more prayers they would promise to say on behalf of the dead relatives of the donors, to get them out of limbo.

So although many Halloween traditions have pagan origins, the practice of trick-or-treating actually evolved from a medieval form of prayer-extortion. Likewise, the jack-o-lantern is derived from a medieval Irish folk tale, but is also deeply Christian. A man named

Jack, notorious as a drunkard and a trickster, tricked Satan into climbing a tree, then carved an image of a cross in the tree's trunk, trapping the devil up the tree. When he died, Jack was denied entrance to heaven because of his evil ways, but also to hell, because he had tricked the devil. As a consolation, the devil gave him a single ember to light his way in the frigid darkness of limbo. He put the ember inside a hollowed-out turnip so it would last longer.

Which is a useful cautionary tale for kids: Don't try to trick the devil! Of course, there are other reasons for fearing Halloween: razor blades in candy apples, crack cocaine in pixie sticks, etc. But according to at least one expert, Joel Best, a sociologist from the University of Delaware, they're all as big a myth as Santa Claus. He scanned every major newspaper from 1958 to 1998 looking for stories about blades in apples and poisoned Milk Duds. He analyzed about a hundred articles, and followed up with phone calls to police and hospitals. His conclusion: the number of kids critically injured by horrible Halloween deeds was ... zero. "I can't say that it has never happened, but to say that it happens a lot, that it happens all the time... There's just no evidence," he said in an interview.

So, to sum up: a nice, safe, Christian holiday, full of excellent moral lessons for children and parents alike. Anyway, it's fun. More fun than carolling. I'd swallow a poisoned Milk Dud before I'd do that again.

Holiday Recall

MEMORIES OF (MOSTLY) MERRY CHILDHOOD FESTIVITIES RESTORE
SEASONAL CHEER TO WRITER DOUGLAS BELL.

Christmas. What to say? At a certain point in your life, after
birth, after death, after divorce, after certain forms of rap music start to
annoy, after-after-after, Yuletide seems what the philosophers refer to as
overdetermined. Which is a fancy way of saying the whole subject bores
you witless. But then, just when you seem to be settling into a Grinch-like
sulk, something restores your sense of proportion, and you are into it.
For me, it's always the tree.

    Most years, my children and I go out to a farm north of Toronto
and cut down our very own evergreen, stuff it in the back of the station
wagon and clatter home with the kids howling mock versions of "Jingle
Bells" ("Jingle Bells, Santa smells, Rudolph took ballet"). A day or two
later, the decorations are hooked on: lights, baubles and tinsel, topped by a

Christmas angel placed by my five-year-old, teetering atop a shaky stepladder.

I hold my breath.

The whole performance strikes me as a down-market version of my own childhood memories. This leaves me with the all-too-familiar sensation that somehow I'm failing to live up to standards of Christmas past, thus dooming my children to an increasingly dismal Christmas future.

Still, on the day, the memories flood in, and suddenly I'm seven years old, standing at the front door of my grandparents' majestic house in midtown Toronto's Wychwood Park. It's Christmas Night. The enormous oak door swings open, and the first thing I see is one of those weirdly distorted fish-eye mirrors in the front hall, decorated with festive red bows and varieties of Christmas vegetation. Coats are dispensed to a small white-haired man in a white jacket known to the family only as "Colbeck" (I didn't learn that his first name was Ted until he was long dead). The grown-ups move swiftly to join in pre-dinner drinks and the weary "how did we get through another Christmas" conversation. I move into an enormous panelled drawing room. The ceiling is two floors up, with a second-floor balcony halfway up the north wall. My eyes are drawn to one corner, where stands, framed by enormous leaded-glass windows, a magnificent Maritime spruce that had been mailed the week before from New Brunswick. That's right, I said mailed.

Now I know that the better word would be "shipped," since obviously the connotations of the word "mailed" suggest a postie lugging a huge tree along snow-covered streets and stuffing the thing through the mail slot. Though that having been said, as a seven-year-old that was my impression.

In my mind's eye, I saw George Lee, who managed my grandparents' property in St. Andrews, wandering into the local post office. George, a grizzled realist with a sentimental side, would grumble at having to once again mail Mrs. Ambridge's 20-foot-tall Christmas tree to Toronto. Then there would be the whole business of actually having to wrap the tree with that brown paper, then getting enough stamps on the package to get it there.

As I stood there looking at the riot of decorations set amidst the tree's wide evergreen wingspan, I'd start to feel this warm sensation, a sort of culmination-of-Christmas moment. That lingering look would fade as dinner asserted itself in earnest. The table ran the length of the drawing room. Everything seemed to glitter — silverware, glass and the shiny wrapping around the Christmas crackers. We'd start with smoked salmon served with black bread and capers. Then, seemingly seconds after we'd started, Granny would feel around with her foot for a buzzer hidden under the table, and a steady stream of uniformed servants would sweep among us, replacing smaller plates with dishes the size of manhole covers. This was the turkey bit. The bird, subject of all conversation during the course of the meal, was immense. The issue was always how long did it take to cook? And at what temperature, pray tell?

You wouldn't think that would be enough to sustain an entire evening's discussion, but it did. Beyond the turkey, the mashed potatoes, the peas, the stuffing, there was mashed turnip, known as rutabaga. Which I didn't like. Say it a few times — "rutabaga, rutabaga, rutabaga." Now imagine something that tastes as bad as that sounds.

"Douglas," my sweet, determined, ever-so-slightly controlling Granny would say. "Wouldn't you like some rutabaga? It's delicious."

"I-I-uh, well, ummm if you say so, Granny." It was all I could do not to gag.

Eventually, the main course dishes were shuttled out, and a buzz of anticipation came over the table. Plum pudding was coming, and, for a moment at least, it would be on fire. Accompanying the pyrotechnics was Champagne. Not just any Champagne, mind, but Bollinger, on account

102

of that was "what Churchill drank." What qualification the greatest wartime leader the world has ever known had for discerning sparkling wines was unclear, but everyone nodded sagely nonetheless. In the midst of this the Christmas crackers appeared. These were long cylinders wrapped in shiny paper. Each end had a narrow strip of paper tucked inside an open-ended sleeve. The ritual dictated that you and your seatmate would each grab one end and pull. This would result in a tiny explosion followed by the acrid smell of gunpowder. The one left holding the cracker would, in effect, win the contents. This usually included a paper crown, some bauble or other, and the inevitable Christmas joke, which you'd have to read to the assembled. These jokes were so corny I can't repeat them here. OK ... maybe just one.

What do you call a doctor who treats ducks?

A real quack.

Then, of course, you'd have to repeat the joke in French.

Très amusant.

In the midst of this lunacy, there always seemed to be a couple of guests from way outside the box. One year I remember there appeared a couple who were some sort of Italian nobility trapped somehow in Toronto for Christmas. They were both strikingly attractive and armed with deep reserves of charm. As the evening wore on, I remember they looked slightly agog at one another, confronted with all this WASP ritual. I remember thinking then that there must be a much bigger world away from the confines of Wychwood Park, where the trappings of our Christmas might seem a trifle odd or eccentric. But that feeling soon passed, and I was back to filling up my memory with the ballast of Christmas past. The way Christmas is supposed to be.

Getting Sorted

SARAH HAMPSON FINDS A BALANCE BETWEEN THE JOBS OF
WRITER AND MOTHER.

I blame it all on laundry. The fact that I'm a writer, I mean.
Because no matter how often I imagine some very romantic reason, like,
I don't know, needing to make sense of the world or something, I feel my
inner self shaking her head and a voice tsk-tsking, scolding me for being so
dishonest. If it were about some lofty ideal, that voice peevishly points
out, you'd have felt compelled to do it far sooner than you did. As it is, I
didn't start my life as a writer until about 10 years ago. I was an ad chick
then, an associate creative director in a large international advertising
agency, well paid and quick on the draw with slogans.

A successful pitch to a client and our team would swagger out of
the boardroom, blowing smoke from the barrels of our imaginary guns.
I was living that have-it-all life. Three children, all boys, under the age of

five. A nice house. A nanny. A Jeep Cherokee. A magazine life, really, complete with designer window treatments. But there was laundry. And by that I mean not just the real dirty stuff, but the messiness of my various responsibilities, their interconnections, their frustrations, and my per-ceived failures to meet them, all of which I tried really hard to, er, wash right out of my life. I hadn't embraced my inner laundry, I guess you could say, and I had to go home, to be home, to sort it all out and put it in the right places.

There are people, other professional mothers, who would argue that all that having a dual home-and-office life requires is organization. Have schedules. Plan meals. Hire the perfect nanny. And for a few years, I did that. There is something about having children that makes you think it's all manageable if only you can keep things in bins.

Not just toys and paired mittens, but responsibilities as well. Maybe it's because babies and toddlers can be dressed up so perfectly, and without complaint. They're like well-coordinated accent pillows or something. They fit perfectly in that beautifully designed magazine life.

But it became clear to me that I wasn't really living my life, compart-mentalized like that and however well organized I was. I was on the out-side of both, an observer and manager of them rather than an inhabitant of either. I would be sitting at work, thinking about whether Nicholas, the eldest boy, had come home for lunch yet and if he had fought with his brother, Tait, over that dinky toy they both loved so much. Luke, the youngest, was then just a baby, manageable and sweet, but I found myself thinking about him during the day in the same way I was once unable to get boyfriends out of my mind.

When I was on a television commercial shoot in Sydney, Australia, I remember thinking, as the creative team hung out on Bondi Beach for a whole day waiting for a casting session to be organized, that I was on

holiday with people I didn't want to be on holiday with. You know something's wrong when you're twentysomething, on a beach, still bikini-worthy, and your mind is not on your tan.

So I quit and decided to work freelance from home. For a time, we kept the nanny, and I maintained a small office outside of the house, in my husband's downtown Toronto building. The idea was that I could balance home and office more easily if I was working for myself. But I still maintained that separation from home because our house was small, and the children were too young to understand the meaning of a closed door, let alone the shift in my identity from mommy to professional. It was a fantasy born of reading the diaries of Anne Morrow Lindbergh, I think. The wife of Charles Lindbergh, the aviation hero, she lived a charmed but busy life as a mother and as a writer. She moved between the two by crossing the green lawns of her garden to a writing cottage situated at the far end of the property. My trip across my garden was a 15-minute drive in my car.

It worked, but not for long.

The decision to truly face my responsibilities as a parent and to myself (for I always saw work as something I was not only doing to help support my family but also as a sanity outlet) happened on the day our nanny, our third in five years, decided to leave. My husband withheld the news from me for as long as he could. With the children, I had stayed on an extra week at a cottage we rented for a few weeks in the summer. He came up for the last couple of days, and on the night before we were to drive home, he told me what our nanny had announced to him a week earlier. I cried, wept actually, not because she was so great a caregiver, but because I knew I had to take on the task of making it all work.

And thus began my quest to take my life out of its various bins, to disorganize my life a little bit. We didn't hire another nanny. The older two boys were in school full-time by then. I arranged for them to stay there for lunch. Luke was in playschool for half a day. I enrolled him for the full day. From nine in the morning until almost four, silence reigned in my household. At that point my work had evolved more into magazine and newspaper journalism than corporate writing or advertising. Which meant there were fewer meetings and more time spent in front of a computer, alone. We bought a larger house, a great heap of a house that was far from perfect but had more room, an office for me on the second floor and bedrooms on a third level for the children.

Soon after we moved in, I remember standing in the backyard, raking leaves in the autumn, content in the way true contentedness comes to you, slowly, unconsciously, creeping into your bones like sunshine across a patio. I am standing in the centre of my life, I thought, and all of it, my job as a journalist, as a mother, as a wife, revolves around me.

It's like being in the eye of a storm, where it's calm. And I realized that, for the first time, I was beginning to think of my house, not so much as a stage setting for the movie of our family life, but as a place that housed a collection of personalities, ambitions and needs, all of it messy and lovely and too big to be contained by the urge to organize.

Now, six years in, I have found a balance that works. And none of it is scripted. I can do none of this separation of work and personal life that so many others prescribe. I do not walk around the block after the children have left and re-enter my house as if it were an office. (Someone's suggestion.) I do not get properly dressed in work clothes to help draw a line between the two worlds. Maybe because I love the way the two complement each other. As a mother, I must be completely present. When a child wants a cookie, he or she wants a cookie. Now, or else. Of course, teenagers, which my first two boys are now, understand the idea of waiting until I have the time to do something, but they still need me, there and listening, when they come in the door after school. Conversely, as a writer, I must withdraw. I must be absent, lost for hours on end, inside my own head. Living like this, in one house but in two worlds, is not, as some might think, like straddling two galloping horses. It's as simple as crossing thresholds. Like going from the kitchen to the shower. Or from the play-room to the bedroom. One is an escape from the other.

And sometimes, the fact that the two worlds exist side by side is an advantage. They can inform each other. Once, Steve Martin, the actor and comedian, called while I was sitting at my desk, dressed in sweats, munch-ing on a snack. It was the real domestic me barking a hello as I answered the phone.

"Oh hi," he said casually. "It's Steve Martin."

A telephone interview had been arranged by his publicist in New York. But he had phoned half an hour early, catching me off guard.

I apologized for sounding so abrupt and quickly adopted the voice of a solicitous journalist. It was weird, talking to Steve Martin at my desk that looks out over my street, with the music of my teenagers barely muffled behind their doors one floor up and with my golden retriever curled up at my feet.

Weird and wonderful. Because the fact that I was at home made me feel at home, and thus rendered the entire conversation more casual, as if I had someone I knew on the line. He, too, was at home, at home in Hollywood, so when I asked what it was like in L.A., he told me it had been one of the most beautiful days of the fall, clear and warm, and that he was just now watching the sun go down behind his house. He sounded dreamy and relaxed, not the wisecracking performer I somehow expected. The next day, I had to reach him again to clarify some of his quotes. It was the morning, so I asked if he was in his pajamas.

"My yoga outfit, actually," he chuckled. After we had spoken for 15 minutes, his doorbell rang, and his dogs barked. His yoga instructor had arrived. I had been given a glimpse of the domestic side of Steve Martin, and all because we had been talking from our homes.

Of course, there are times I wish for more of a separation between home and work. One incident in particular comes to mind. I had been out, running an errand, and left Tait, who is 14, at home with instructions to answer the phone. When I returned, I asked him if anyone had called.

"Oh yes," he said. "There was someone." From his pocket, he pulled out a crumpled piece of paper on which he had scribbled a message.

"Someone about Tony Bannett?" he asked, hoping I would know who he meant.

"Who?" I said.

"Tony Bannett?" he wondered again.

"Not someone about Tony Bennett," I said with horror in my voice. I had been waiting to hear from one of His People if an interview could be scheduled for the following week.

"Yeah! That's it," Tait exclaimed, pleased he hadn't totally messed up.

I took a playful swipe at his shoulder, and he sloped off to the kitchen for a snack in the way only a 14-year-old who is six-feet-three-inches tall can slope. "So who is Tony Bennett anyway?" he asked between mouthfuls of peanut butter sandwich.

A sigh was all I could manage.

Sugar Beets & Roses

KRISTEN DEN HARTOG NOURISHES A DEEP-ROOTED
FLOWER FANCY.

My frontyard in downtown Toronto is covered with dirty white stones. Beneath them lies a layer of black landscaping fabric, and beneath that, soil. So you see, though it is April, nothing will grow here other than the lone maple tree that shoots up from the centre of the yard. Because of the maple, and my swoony, melancholy nature, fall is my favourite season. The leaves in their varying shades drop into the yard and cover the dirty white stones, but in spring, every ugly pebble is visible. My frontyard is approximately 10 feet by 15 feet. I have never measured it in the conventional way, but I can imagine two of me lying along the front of the yard and three of me along the side, so I know. A little red fence runs around the edges, perhaps to contain the stones. I don't mind the yard's size, but I do mind its stones, so uniform, so numerous they

110

might be chips of Styrofoam. Which would be better, come to think of it, because wind alone could erase them, at least from my yard. If this were my home, not a rented one, the stones would be the first to go. The smothering black fabric would be lifted, and the soil would be tilled. Ferns would unfurl in the shade, and every possible herb would stretch out to the sun. A tiny postage stamp of green. Such a garden would have made my Opa smile.

The rocks, however, would have horrified him. For most of his life, he was a gardener. I get my Dutch green thumb from him, thwarted though it is. When I first began working as a florist, 10 years ago, I wished he could know, but he had died years before.

Prior to, during and after the war, he grew vegetables in his little town in Holland, and sold them at market in The Hague. While the world was falling apart, he was growing melons, endive, asparagus, beets, carrots, onions, radishes, cabbages and potatoes. His garden was enormous. I can't imagine how many of me might have fit along its width and length. In the poorest winters, Opa kept his family alive on a diet of sugar beets, all that was left over, food grown for pigs. By day he was a gardener, and by night a hero working for the Resistance movement. (Of course, he would never have put it that way.) Beneath the floorboards of his home lay a wireless radio, like a secret plant Opa tended. The radio gave him news of his missions. Once German soldiers appeared at their front door, looking for him, but he escaped out the back and was spared. I have known these stories forever, but still, as I write this, I cannot imagine him in such a role. With his bushy eyebrows furrowed, and the radio pressed up to his very long ear. To me, he is and always has been simply a gardener. But perhaps he is the epitome of gardeners, because growers of things should be people who not only despise but rebel against cruelty. I know a woman who can't kill the slugs that ooze into her garden, and I hope when

111

I have a garden I will not kill slugs either, or make them drink beer or cover their fleshy bodies with salt. I don't know what Opa would have said to this. Though he was kind, he was much more pragmatic than I am.

When the war was almost over, the bombs came. Opa heard the planes in the near distance. He went to the window and yelled, "Hurry, come home!" because his sons were playing close by. He could see them running, but it was too late. My father lost his leg and my uncle lost his arm. Still, the garden was replanted. The war ended, and Opa once again became a gardener by day, and a husband and father by night. He may have continued that way had his garden not been paved to make a highway.

In 1951, he came with his family to Aylmer, Ontario. His first brief job was as a farmhand. He, my Oma, my father and his siblings (five children in all) lived in a tiny hut on the farm. The farmer was rude, but Opa remained silent. He did his work. He fed his family. One day the farmer was milking a cow, and the cow's calf kicked over the pail, and the milk spilled onto the ground. The farmer grabbed a piece of wood. He beat the calf until it lay still and bleeding. Opa packed up his family and their belongings. They left immediately.

The Dutch Reformed Church in their area took them in, and Opa quickly found a job at a local nursery, where he worked until he retired. They thought his thumb was not only green, but magic. He was able to make the trollius flourish when no one else could. His body of knowledge grew too. Roses and exotic indoor plants became his specialty. Hibiscus was his favourite, and it remains my own father's favourite for just that reason. As a child, I could not see out the window of their home for all the plants that lived at my eye level. Across the street there was a cornfield that went on forever, and in the yard there were rosebushes. I did not know they had any effect on me at the time. I stuck my nose into the open blooms and smelled them, but other than that I was not particularly interested in flowers, or in plants. In fact, I probably became less interested the older I got. By the time I was a teenager, I was writing a lot, but I doubt a flower ever appeared in those stories, which were for the most part about New York City prostitutes with names like Imogene, or runaway pregnant teenagers. "Her stomach swelled like a beach ball." I wrote reams of melodramatic poetry, and I drew accompanying pictures of girls with blood for tears. Flowers were very far from my mind.

When Opa retired from the nursery, they gave him a party and a reclining chair. At home, he tended his roses and his treasured indoor garden. When I was 17 he died of cancer. I visited him in the hospital during his last days. I was very thin then, for my own teenage reasons. I remember that I leaned forward to kiss his gaunt face, and I rested my head on his shoulder. I looked down at our arms, side by side, and I saw that his was thinner than mine.

Years later, I became a florist by happy accident. I needed an enjoyable job that I could leave behind at the end of the day, so that when I came home I could write fiction. (I didn't count on Valentine's Day, Mother's Day and Christmas, aching hands, cedar-scraped skin and wedding stress, but that's another story.) I answered an ad that said, "Creative help wanted for flower shop. No formal experience necessary." I knew absolutely nothing, but I learned. And I knew Opa would be pleased if he could see me. Even in Canada, the floral business is full of Dutch people, and often I'd receive the comment, "This work is in your genes." It wasn't my career of choice, but I loved it. I worked for 10 years in the industry, and have only recently left to write full time. What I hadn't imagined was that the florist part of me would so affect the writer part of me. My gardens have always been pots on steps, but roses, wildflowers and the bugs that eat them live in the pages of *Water Wings,* my first book. In my second, a novel intertwined with fables, a girl fastens peonies to her spiderweb hair. Right now I'm at work on a children's story: it's about a wildflower, William Trillium, who accidentally moves to the city on the leg of a picnic table, and must adjust to a cosmopolitan, sparsely starred world. Something I know a little about: small-town girl in the big city.

One of my sisters still lives in Deep River, Ontario, the town where we grew up. She and her husband and sons have a sprawling piece of property outside of town, and an enormous rock-free garden thrives in their backyard. Like Opa, she feeds her family with the vegetables she grows there. The tiniest man lives in that garden. He is what my family calls the *kaboutertje*, but in English we'd call him a garden gnome. He has a red hat and pants, a blue shirt and a long white beard. He belongs to my nephew Ethan now, but he came from my Opa's garden — which would be funny to you if you knew Opa, because Opa was not at all a garden-gnome kind of man. Nothing about him was frivolous. The *kaboutertje* was given to him by neighbours who were building a pool. The only way the bulldozers and cement pourers could access the neighbours' yard was through Opa's, and he had given his consent, though surely the modern, lavish act of building a pool must have been bewildering to him, a man from a different world. After the ordeal was over, the neighbours, knowing Opa was a gardener, presented him with the little man. And though Opa was no gnome lover, he was touched by the gift — by the fact that someone had given him something. It sat in his garden for years. For the rest of his life, in fact, and then for the rest of Oma's. To me the *kaboutertje* would be ugly, even a bit disturbing, without the story that comes with him. With the story, he is a family treasure, and a reminder of a fine man who grew things.

114

Land Roving

TEA AND TURF FUEL BARBARA MCLEAN'S TIME IN IRELAND'S SOFT COUNTRYSIDE.

If clouds are just so on a late summer day, heavy dark satin draped over wet gossamer underskirts, I can look out my farm kitchen window and imagine myself back on the west coast of Ireland. The rolling hills are reminiscent, the stone walls look similar in shadow, and soft sheep season every field they graze like distant grains of salt.

The biggest difference is the reluctance of a continental Canadian sky to clear quickly. In Ireland, the sun bursts its way through boiling clouds, if only momentarily, and the weather is constantly in flux.

It was 1972. We were young, unencumbered and looking for adventure. After hitchhiking from Victoria to St. John's, we hopped a flight from Gander, Newfoundland, to Prestwick, Scotland, stuck out our other thumbs, begged our way south and ferried across the Irish Sea. From Dublin we hiked and hitched to County Sligo, where a friend of a friend had a 300-year-old cottage on the coast. It was the most formative stay of our lives.

For months we had been freecampers, used to pitching our Canadian Tire pup tent on prairie or rock or moor. We ate what we could carry, cold bread and cheese, fruit, bought hot tea and soup from roadside cafés, but nowhere could we cook real meals or stock up on supplies. Road-weary, we were ready to settle for a bit.

Ready to dig in and domesticate, to rest, to ponder the next step.

As recent graduates, we'd spent years in labs and lecture halls, with artificial light, with jargon, with microscopes and magnifying glasses searching for the fatal flaw in a human cell, the distinctive brush stroke in a famous painting. We worked in concrete buildings with escalators, green space only a distant view, rarely a fragrant soft surface to tread. Wandering was welcome therapy to our city-worn hearts, but the land's end on the Irish coast slowed us down, let us experience life with nothing more artificial than a matchstick to light the fagots in the stove.

The cottage was stone, its walls so thick the sills of the small windows were as wide as tables. The roof was thatch, thick straw tied in bunches by craftsmen who knew how to use what grew around them. Rain softly rolled off the packed stems, making no sound.

Even hail bounced in silence. But when the sun returned, the roof steamed with warmth, and the thatch glowed.

The inviting hearth edged an open turf fire that filled one end of the cottage. The chimney hung wide above the grate and andirons, with pothooks hanging from its depths to hold the black kettle and the flat griddle. We had never seen blocks of turf before, had known nothing of them. The Canadian fires we remembered used the riches of soft cedar kindling, birch bark and twigs to quicken the dry maple of our forests, cut and split and stored in a woodshed. Fire-making was easy on the summer-cottage-days of childhood. But turf is carved into bricks from the great peat bogs of Ireland, stacked like cordwood to dry in a countryside constantly barraged with showers and storms from wet westerly winds off the sea. It smells heavenly when you get it going, but even with a bit of dryish gorse underneath it fizzled out like damp mould at our early efforts. It was the first task we had to learn to live there.

Overwhelmed with the need to make things after so much roving, I craved to create comforts and substance from raw ingredients. We found our way to the town of Sligo and bought supplies. Yeast for bread, paraffin wax for sealing jam jars, wool for knitting, and books.

This was not an easy task. Powdered yeast did not exist. We were sent to the bakery by quizzical shopkeepers and instructed there on the use of fresh-pressed yeast. Paraffin in Ireland is what we call kerosene, so we were misunderstood in our intention to use it with preserves. Books, however, and wool were clear. They are languages that translate well across oceans. Woollen yarn creates its own communication on the needles of Irish fishing families, who knit distinct personal patterns in the cables of loved ones' sweaters. They speak tragic paragraphs in times of loss, when only the identifying wool washes ashore after a violent storm.

On the wettest days, we stayed in the cottage, boiling the kettle over the turf for tea, knitting socks, reading poetry and local history, forming loaves of rough bread to rise by the fire. I experienced the peace that Yeats said "comes dropping slow / dropping from the veils of the morning" and saw what the poet saw, the "noon a purple glow," and heard not lake water, but the sea "lapping with low sounds by the shore." When the rain was sporadic, or misty — what the Irish call a "soft" day — we ventured to the water's edge, watched the tides so foreign to Ontarians.

At low tide, we learned to gather mussels, bring them back to steam open over the turf for a succulent supper, garnished with tiny pearls. We baked Irish shortcakes on the griddle. Flour mixed with lard, dotted with currants, rolled and cut into rounds, flipped over the peat and laced with its scent. And there were potatoes. Until then potatoes were always an adjunct for me.

They were the medium for the real message of butter, gravy or sauce. But in Ireland potatoes have a taste that bursts in the mouth. Tender, exotic, rich with flavour and texture, they bear no resemblance to the lumpen fodder I had purchased in heavy paper bags with string mesh windows in the grocery store back home. These were growing tubers, freshly harvested from the rich earth, their skins red and gold and thin as gauze.

We learned how they grew, followed the thin root leads underground to the prize and left the plant to grow more. And we learned about the years they did not grow but rotted in the ground while the people starved. The cottage, part of a thriving village before the famine, was the sole survivor of a lost community.

The garden flourished with good potatoes now, and rhubarb and gooseberries for my jam, which I left on the shelves as meagre rent. I walked the stone garden wall to pick the berries and, not knowing they had thorns, suffered when I lost my footing and fell in the bushes.

We walked the hills and fields, marvelling always at the skies, which constantly moved and swayed and argued over whether to be wet or fair. Anoraks on and then off, our bodies chilled and then warm, but always there was a breeze to dry out after the sudden soaking. Across the flats was the big house, memory of times past in an Anglo-Irish world.

We were invited for dinner to this mansion, which had no electricity but was lit with candles and lamps. It had huge rooms, a grand piano and

119

bellpulls to summon servants, whose ghosts no longer heeded the calls. A massive Aga cooker roasted the meal, and 23 of us sat, uncrowded, around the Victorian table. Potatoes were served in three different ways.

The extended family of the friend of our friend kindly taught us the lore of the land, and the land itself, the mountains of Ben Bulben and Knocknarea, the beaches of Sligo Bay, where we boiled water for tea in a billy and had proper sandwiches and scones with jam, whipped by winds that brought in showers of sand and hail.

But the most wondrous thing of all was the solitude of that place. We lived mainly off the land, the produce in the garden and orchards that others had planted and tended, and the wild food of the tide. We learned that we could live in quiet and isolation. We learned that we could love a garden and harvest and transform its produce into succulent simple dishes that would feed us in more ways than we imagined possible.

Eventually we had to carry on, proceed in our travels to cities and pavements and grey buildings beyond. But it kept us going until we returned to Ontario to find our own land and start our own country life. As it did for Yeats, the lush Irish countryside stayed with us through the harsh times "in the deep heart's core" and carried us through.

And now in Grey County, where I raise sheep and chickens and grow a garden of my own, I realize how important those magic weeks were in directing us back to the land and showing us a way to live. Around Sligo Bay there is an expression that says if the clouds clear long enough so that you can see the shape of Knocknarea, it is about to rain. As I look out my Canadian kitchen window on a late summer morning, if the clouds are just so, I can imagine Knocknarea just behind that rainburst. I can almost convince myself it is waiting to reappear in a momentary gust of wind, swirling in off the faraway sea.

Holiday Home

CHARLOTTE GRAY RETREATS TO HER TRANQUIL PINE ISLAND
COTTAGE EVEN ON THE COLDEST WINTER DAY.

Two white pines, each more than 60 metres high, dominate the
view from the window of our cottage. The trunk of the one on the left is
plumb-straight: 200 years ago, it would have been felled by
a lumberman eager to feed the British Navy's appetite for naval masts.
Today, however, the pine trunk is black, bare and very dead, victim of a
porcupine's appetite for its bark. The tree on the right, however, is covered
in glossy green needles and its crown is heavy with new growth. A gust of
wind sends ripples through the foliage that remind me of the soft waves
I send through my duvet as I shake it out each morning.

A narrow, shallow inlet lies on the far side of the white pines. A layer
of lilies covers its surface and a forest of water weeds lurks below. Beyond
the inlet is the peninsula — a thin strip of rock along which pines and

junipers straggle in single file. The tip of the peninsula is dominated by a pair of ospreys, which annually returns to its lofty, untidy nest to produce a noisy youngster. And visible beyond the peninsula is first the lake, glistening in the sunlight, and finally the next cluster of islands. Trees, water, trees, water, more trees — and then the sky.

The spectacular vista that I enjoy across Newboro Lake, north of Kingston, is almost a parody of Tom Thomson's iconic windblown pines. The lily-laden inlet has the misty appeal of one of Monet's Giverny paintings. I sit at my desk, mesmerized by the play of sun on water and the sound of the baby osprey demanding lunch. I feel completely at home, lapped by the tranquility, at peace with myself. But can I claim this as "home": the mythic space in which I feel the most intense sense of belonging?

"Home," for most people, signifies some childhood place, heavy with memories: my family has owned this island cottage for only two years. Yet it has become an instant "home" for me, partly because, like many immigrants to Canada, I have a confused sense of what "home" signifies. In Canada, when I talk of "going home," I mean visiting the country of my birth. In England, mention of "home" means Ottawa, where I have lived for the past 22 years. I feel more Canadian than British these days, rooted in this country by the day-to-day reality of Canadian family and friends. The transition point in identity comes with the shift in primary loyalty from the past generation to the future, from parents in the old country to children in the new one. Yet at night, scenes from that other life, in an English boarding school or the damp little house I owned in Kentish Town, London, rise to the surface of my dreams, pulling me back to an earlier sensibility. For most of my adult life, I have been uncertain about "where is home?"

Charlotte Gray

Now I have a home. The appeal of our summer cottage is beyond aesthetics — although I challenge anyone to define a more picturesque scene than an old log building overlooking a still lake in the heat of an Ontario July day. The emotional tug that our cottage exerts for me has to do with the nature of cottages in the Canadian psyche, as the multi-generational anchor in a rapidly changing world. It is about "the cottage" not as physical place, but as a state of mind.

Back in England, the term "cottage" simply referred to a building that was smaller than a house but prettier than a shack. Family friends who had a holiday home as well as a city house would talk possessively about their "little place" or their "hideaway" in the hills or on the coast of Scotland or Wales. No single term covered every kind of private rural retreat. Anyway, few British people own two houses — which is hardly surprising considering the astronomical property prices everywhere in the U.K. British conversations about second domiciles consist of weary tales about local taxes, medieval drains and creeping dry rot rather than sentimental chat about community barbecues and Aunt Barbara's pasta salad.

The British do have one generic escape similar to Canadians' cottages: the seaside. My family always talked of "going to the seaside," as though being by the sea was a state of mind rather than a destination with geographic coordinates. But as anybody who has visited Blackpool, Bridlington or Brighton on an August weekend knows, there is nothing private about the beach — or even, given British summer weather, pleasant.

So my first summer in Canada, I was confused by the constant references to "the cottage." I had never heard the word used like this. Whose cottage? I wondered. Was everybody converging on the same cottage, somewhere in the backwoods? Even in the grocery store, as I quickly learnt to call the local shop, the sales staff would ask me if

I was going to "the cottage," as though they personally knew my private hideaway. At that stage, I didn't even have a cottage. But I had an uneasy feeling that everybody else did, and I was somehow being excluded from this national ritual.

However, after 20 years of renting properties for the summer, I joined the national statistic: the roughly 50 percent of Canadians who have a place of their own to go in the summer. (In Northern Ontario and Alberta, it seems to be "the camp": in Newfoundland and British Columbia, it's "the cabin.") My husband and I found an old log lodge on an island in an undeveloped lake, and we threw ourselves into the joys of rustic furniture, saggy beds and rural flea markets. Our three sons, on the cusp of manhood, discovered the excitement of chainsaws and motorboats. We all bonded with our new island home, and incidentally rebonded with each other.

These days, I know viscerally as well as intellectually that a Canadian cottage is much more than a holiday home. It is a place where the owners take the most pleasure in each other's company, be it an intimate twosome or a sprawl of arthritic matriarchs, chattering aunts and barefoot cousins. Of course, family meltdowns are as common in cottage country as in the suburbs: questions about who bent the boat propeller or lost the pickaxe can get nasty fast. But the most important aspect of Canadian cottages is that you are all there. In my own case, this means that my husband and I spend uninterrupted time during summer weekends with our sons, aged 21, 19 and 16. We have shared projects, such as construction of a dock, clearing deadwood out of the inlet, and acquisition of necessary supplies of beer. The rhythm of life is slower when you are insulated from urban pressures by an unreliable cell phone and encircling waters. We are rarely alone: any number of university buddies, hockey mates and girlfriends join the fun. But nobody leaves when the sun goes down: I drift off to bed

Charlotte Gray

while others disappear to the campfire or embark on knife-edge games of Risk and Monopoly.

So in two short years, "the cottage" has become home for me as, over the past 50 or 70 years, it has for so many Canadian families. My husband and I know that our sons will spend little more time in our Ottawa house: two are at university over 2,000 kilometres away, and the youngest is already chafing to spend a year in Europe. But they will flock back to the island each summer, along with the nesting ospreys.

The old log building was never built for winter occupation: sharp drafts slice in through rattling casements, and a blazing fire in the huge fieldstone fireplace warms a radius of only two metres. By November we have put the shutters on the lodge, turned off the water supply and packed the bedding into plastic boxes to protect it from mice. We may walk across the frozen lake in February, to check the doors are still locked and to burn piles of dead wood on the ice.

Yet our Pine Island retreat has become home in a more metaphysical way, too. On dark, cold days, our island cottage continues to sit centre stage in my psyche as "home." Through the winter, I sit at my keyboard in the city, close my eyes, and think of those two tall pines, swaying in the wind. I hear the ospreys calling to each other. To escape the stress of deadlines or traffic jams, I allow my mind to drift to the lilies in the inlet and the sparkle of the lake beyond the peninsula. I watch the blue heron flying low along the shoreline of the next island. At night, I can almost imagine that cars racing past our house are distant motorboats. Half-awake at dawn, I pretend to myself that I'll open my eyes to see hummingbirds at the feeder, rather than my husband reading the morning newspaper as he gets ready for the office. "The cottage" is embedded in my imagination. It is the place I dream about.

126

INDEX

All *Notes from Home* were originally published in
Canadian House & Home magazine.
Thank you to all of these authors, who have kindly given us
permission to reprint the following stories: